GOLD, FRANKENSTEIN AND MANURE

Ivor Wynne Jones

Llechwedd Publications
1997

Gold, Frankenstein and manure

© Ivor Wynne Jones, 1997
ISBN 0-905935-21-7

Letters of the Victorian slate maker
John Whitehead Greaves
liberally annotated a sesquicentenary later
by Ivor Wynne Jones

Published by   Llechwedd Publications,
Llechwedd Slate Caverns,
Blaenau Ffestiniog,
Gwynedd LL41 3NB

Tel: 01766 830306

The arrival of J.W.Greaves

JOHN WHITEHEAD GREAVES was 23 years of age when he left the family home at Barford, Warwickshire, in 1830, to seek his fortune. His elder brothers Richard (born 1802) and Edward (1803) had been taken into family banking businesses in Warwick and Leamington from the age of 16, but John was advised to try his luck in the colonies - as was his younger brother Joseph, who went to New Zealand (but was back in Warwickshire by 1862).

J.W.Greaves got no farther west than Caernarfon Slate Quay, built as a pioneering job-creation project initiated by the enterprising town Mayor, the first Marquess of Anglesey, to provide work for unemployed soldiers who had fought with him in the Napoleonic wars (in which he lost a leg, commanding the cavalry at Waterloo). They were put to work removing a once-fortified hill which rose out of what is now Castle Square, using the spoil to build the present tidal quay beside the River Seiont.

Needing no persuasion to put off the misery of a long voyage in the squalor, gloom and stench of the accommodation offered to Caernarfon emigrants,[1] Greaves was much attracted by the commercial excitement of the reborn port's golden age. Quite what he did for the next two or three years is something of a mystery, but by 1833 he was in partnership with Edwin Shelton, a wealthy entrepreneur from Worcestershire.

Initially operating two slate quarries in Llanberis, the partners soon concentrated their activities on Blaenau Ffestiniog, first at Bowydd and the adjoining Foty, before beginning mining explorations at Llechwedd in 1846. Shelton left the partnership in 1848, to return to Worcestershire, where he died in 1849[2] - the year when Greaves, on the verge of bankruptcy, discovered the deep slate beds which are still being worked one-and-a-half centuries later, by J.W.Greaves & Sons. It was as good as striking gold and he immediately began to build his own shipping wharf, at a prime spot on the northern side of the new harbour at Porthmadog. He moved his office to the wharf in 1851, and adopted the trade name of *Greaves' Portmadoc Slates®*. Within a decade he doubled his quay space by absorbing the adjoining Canol y Clwt shipyard of Henry Jones. On 23 June 1851 Greaves opened a new letter book, which was meticulously kept by his first shipping clerk, John Thomas.[3]

Greaves (a Quaker) and John Thomas were instrumental in bringing education to the new port, and in establishing the National School, in Snowdon Street.[4] John Thomas and Robert Isaac Jones (Alltud Eifion), of Tremadog, introduced Anglican worship in the Welsh language to Porthmadog, first using the National School to create the congregation for whom St John's church was built during 1873-76.[5] It was effectively a daughter church of St Mary's, built by W.A.Madocks,[6] at Tremadog, in 1806 (though not conveyed to the Church in Wales until 1951)[7], where the customary language of worship was English. The east window at Tremadog church is a memorial to J.W.Greaves and his wife Ellen.[8] John Thomas died, aged 63, on St David's Day, 1887, and John Ernest Greaves, son of J.W.Greaves, attended his funeral at the old Ynyscynhaearn church.[9]

The last ship to collect a cargo of slates at Porthmadog sailed in 1946. The office of J.W.Greaves & Sons remained at Porthmadog until 1969, when it returned to Llechwedd. One of the company's former quayside buildings now houses Porthmadog Maritime Museum.

This volume is an annotated selection from that 1851-53 letter book and associated diaries and accounts of J.W.Greaves and his family.

Porthmadog is born

Porthmadog - originally Port Madoc - was named by and after its creator, William Alexander Madocks (1769-1827). He came to the area with some imaginative land reclamation schemes for the Glaslyn estuary, which he finally enclosed with a mile-long embankment, completed in 1813. It was on the northern edge of this reclaimed land, which used to be flooded by the sea twice a day, that he built Tremadog, which is still a delightful pioneering example of town and country planning. The newly confined waters of the River Glaslyn were (and still are) released twice daily through a sluice, the discharges matching low tides. This regular vigorous scouring created a new deep water channel, which was an unplanned bonus for Madocks. Realising its significance he began to build Porthmadog astride the channel in 1821, and the embryo town was in being by 1824.[10]

Internal railways had been laid at Bowydd as early as 1832 and were in place when Greaves and Shelton acquired the lease.[11] They immediately prepared plans for an 8-mile railway to replace the farm carts which carried their slates from Blaenau Ffestiniog to the traditional quays on the River Dwyryd, probably using the new Gelli Grin quay, midway between Maentwrog and Penrhyndeudraeth.[12] Small boats used to carry the slates from the Dwyryd quays for reloading into ships in the common estuary formed by the Dwyryd and the Glaslyn. Ffestiniog Railway (spelt, until very recently, with a single English "F") had been authorised by Parliament in 1832, but the planning took considerably longer. The 2-ft gauge may have been adopted for maximum co-operation with Greaves and Shelton, whose presence had considerable impact on the project. When a Bill was promoted in 1836 to amend the original Festiniog Railway Act, George Homfray, manager of the Welsh Slate Company's Rhiwbryfdir Lower quarry, told a Parliamentary inquiry that Greaves and Shelton were still contemplating building their own rival railway, which would be available to the Welsh Slate

W.A.MADOCKS 1773-1828

RAILWAY LETTER FEE

F.R. 1p

Company at 4s to 4/6d (20-22½p) a ton. Casson & Co (Thomas and William Casson),[13] at Diffwys quarry, who opposed the 1832 Bill, had also been invited to use the proposed Greaves and Shelton line. Homfray said the project had been delayed only because the partners were undecided whether to route their line to their Dwyryd quay or to the intended Ffestiniog Railway. Another witness said Greaves and Shelton were already tipping in anticipation of laying their railway.[14] They were overtaken by the reality of the new harbour at Porthmadog, and J.W.Greaves was one of

John Whitehead Greaves (1807-1880), founder of Llechwedd Slate Mines.

the guests aboard the first train when Ffestiniog Railway eventually opened on 20 April 1836.

Thus by the time he moved into his Porthmadog office in 1851, Greaves had been using the Ffestiniog Railway for two years to carry his Llechwedd slates to what is still known as Greaves' Wharf. There he dictated his first letter:

Messrs W.C.Lucy & Co.,   *Port Madoc*
Gloucester.   *23rd June 1851*

> *In reply to your post of 21st inst., I have the pleasure to inform you that the person referred to is considered highly respectable and I believe him perfectly for the amount you name. His Banker informed me this morning he would credit him to any amount say to 1,000.*

Caernarfon quayside (above) during its peak as a slate exporting centre, in the 1890s. Greaves's Wharf is clearly visible on the right of the photograph below, taken in 1893 at Porthmadog harbour. One of these Greaves slate warehouses now contains the town's maritime museum.

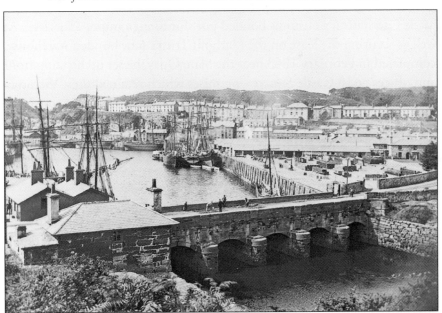

From it we learn that the Royal Mail, relying mostly on horses, could convey a letter from Gloucester to Porthmadog in only two days. The first post office for the area appears to have been opened c1740 at Penmorfa, later subsumed in the new town of Tremadog which became a Penny Post sub-office of Caernarfon in 1840.[15] Porthmadog was not linked to the rail network until 1867, when Cambrian Railways opened the Morfa Mawddach-Pwllheli line.

Also on 23 June Greaves wrote ostensibly from Caernarfon - where he had no office - replying to Richard Ball, of Bristol:

In your letter to Mr Lloyd of 21st inst., you refer to the name of a schooner to be loaded for you, but have not stated what it is. Please let him know this, as well as particulars for bill of lading.

"Mr Lloyd" was the Caernarfon shipping agent Morgan Lloyd, who acted as Greaves' agent in that port for the export of slates from Glynrhonwy quarry, at Llanberis. Morgan Lloyd is best remembered as a wine and spirit merchant, whose prosperity began when the Lords of the Treasury made Caernarfon a customs bonded port for foreign imports in 1842. As well as securing the lease on the Harbour Trust's new bonded warehouse, completed in February 1843 near the Slate Quay, he set up his shop front and offices at 10 Castle Square - premises which retained their Victorian appearance, virtually unchanged, until 1981, when they were converted into the present Morgan Lloyd Tavern.

Glynrhonwy

Glynrhonwy was where Greaves first made an inroad into the slate business, in partnership with Edwin Shelton. The name is confusing in that it has been used, often without further qualification, for separate parts of what was always known to the ground landlords - the successive Barons Newborough - by the generic description of Glynrhonwy farm.[16] At various times the quarried parts of the former farm have been named: Chwarel Bach, Chwarel Fain, Chwarel Fawnog, Chwarel Hir, Chwarel Isaf, Chwarel y Ffordd, Fawnog, Glan y Llyn, Gloddfa Ffordd, Gloddfa Ganol, Glyn Ganol, Glyn Isaf, Glyn Uchaf, Greaves' Quarry, Premier Glynrhonwy, Taylor's Quarry, Twll Clai, Wen Fain - as well as the more familiar Lower Glynrhonwy and Upper Glynrhonwy.[17] There is no longer any obvious demarcation between the different sections.

Situated at the south-eastern end of Padarn lake, Glynrhonwy farm was first worked for slate early in the 18th century. Its finished slates were conveyed by boat, to the northern end of the lake, and on into the marshland then known as Llyn Bogelyn, a small shallow lake which opened up north-west of Penllyn bridge (which was not built until 1825-26).[18] Llyn Bogelyn had a landing stage at Cwm-y-glo, where the slates were transferred to carts for conveyance by unsurfaced road to Caernarfon.

The present Llanberis and Cwm-y-glo bypass was not opened until 1973, using part of the 1869 Caernarfon-Llanberis railway bed. The older Llanberis-Llanrug road, still running through the middle of Cwm-y-glo, was first laid as a tolled turnpike road during 1829-30. Before that, cargoes landed at Cwm-y-glo were taken up the steep hill, due west, which still leads to Bryn Bras Castle (built during 1830-35, and later extended).[19] Near Bryn Bras the road branched either north-west to Llanrug, or southeast, using a reasonably level contour around the side of Cefn Du, which seems to have followed a Roman route to Llanberis Pass, consolidated as a cart track in 1812. Its great advantage was that it avoided the wet land lower down.

The Padarn boats

One of the ancient ferry boats was found in Llyn Padarn in 1977, having sunk some two centuries earlier in 32 feet of water, some 50 yards from the northern shore. Clinker built, with oak planking, it was in good condition despite being laden with 1,354 dressed slates (510 at 20 x 10 inches, and 732 at 16 x 9 inches, plus about 112 broken slates), weighing 1.82 tons. They looked no different from today's product. The slates were packed in neat rows, from side to side of the 5 ft 10 ins wide vessel (maximum beam), which was 19 feet long. It was a flat-bottomed boat, with an iron ring at the bow and a sharply raked stern post, from which a rudder was missing. There was some evidence on the gunwale that the boat may have been steered with a side rudder, suggesting a crew of one, while the boat was towed by a horse on shore.[20]

The boat was raised in January 1978 and is now preserved at the North Wales Slate Museum, Llanberis. John Illsley and Owain T.P.Roberts, of the Welsh Institute of Maritime Archaeology, identified it as being identical in layout and structure (though only two-thirds the size) to three colonial bateaux dating from 1750, and believed to have been made in France, found in Lake George, New York, in 1966. These experts were of the

The raising in 1978 of a boat which sank in Padarn lake, Llanberis, about two centuries earlier, while carrying 1.82 tons of dressed slates.

opinion that the boat was relatively new and in good condition when it sank. They calculated the safe maximum load would be $1^{1}/_{4}$ tons, thus producing the cause of the sinking - gross overloading by more than half-a-ton.[21]

Queen of the lake

Something of the 18th century boatbuilding tradition of Llyn Padarn was recorded by Thomas Pennant:

"The lower lake is about a mile and half long, narrows gradually into the form of a river called Rhythallt, and flows in a diffused channel to Carnarvon, where it assumes the name of Seiont. Near this end of the lake lives a celebrated personage, whom I was disappointed in not finding at home. This is Margaret v[er]ch Evan, of Penllyn, the last specimen of the strength and spirit of the ancient British fair. She is at this time [1786] about 90 years of age. This extraordinary female was the greatest hunter, shooter and fisher of her time. She kept a dozen, at least, of dogs, terriers, greyhounds and spaniels, all excellent in their kinds. She killed more foxes in one year than all the confederate hunts do in ten: rowed stoutly, and was queen of the lake: fiddled excellently, and knew all our old music: did not forget the mechanic arts, for she was a very good joiner: and at the age of 70 was the best wrestler in the country, and few young men dared try a fall with her. Some years ago she had a maid of congenial qualities; but death, that mighty hunter, at last earthed this faithful companion of hers. Margaret was also a blacksmith, shoemaker, boat-builder and maker of harps. She shod her own horses, made her own shoes, and built her own boats, while she was under contract to convey the copper ore down the lakes. I must not forget, that all the neighbouring bards paid their addresses to Margaret, and celebrated her exploits in pure British verse. At length she gave her hand to the most effeminate of her admirers, as if predetermined to maintain the superiority which nature had bestowed on her."[22]

Fach-Wen

Despite at least one published suggestion that Greaves and Shelton worked Lower Glynrhonwy[23], a study of J.W.Greaves's accounts and dates, and a process of elimination, suggests their lease was for Upper Glynrhonwy. Their first Llanberis venture was at Fach-Wen quarry, on a 300-acre site inherited in 1832 by the 3rd Baron Newborough, on the northern side of Padarn lake. Lord Newborough's grandfather, Sir John Wynn, Surveyor of the King's Mines in Wales, had bought it for £800 from the Vaynol Estate, which stretched from the summit of Snowdon to the Menai Straits, and included some of the world's most productive slate deposits (which the estate worked until 1969). Fach-Wen was the exception, in terms of productivity, but it stood astride the route Thomas Assheton-Smith, MP for Caernarvonshire, needed for a railway to convey his Llanberis slates to his harbour at Port Dinorwig. Writing to Lord Newborough in August 1840, Shelton said he was convinced Fach-Wen would never pay without railway communication, and was therefore of value only to Assheton-Smith - who five years later paid Lord Newborough £13,500 for it.

RAF Glynrhonwy

No-one looking at Glynrhonwy today could ever imagine it was once a Royal Air Force station, initially manned by 31 Maintenance Unit. The various quarries were all treated as a single unit - Glynrhonwy farm - when the Air Ministry requisitioned the site three weeks after the outbreak of World War Two. The date is confirmed in a letter[24] written to the Public Trustee, at Bournemouth, on 29 January 1941, by A.J.Wilkins, agent to Colonel R.V.Wynn: "To enable me to obtain a settlement with the tenant who moved out after the Air Ministry had taken over, do you agree that the Ministry will be held responsible for the rent of the farm as from 29 September 1939, since the date of their notice was, I think, 1 January 1940."

The site was converted into a bomb storage depot, and something of the operation was contained in a letter which R.V.Wynn wrote to the Public Trustee on 17 September 1940, when squeezing the maximum rent out of the unexpected windfall for derelict land: "Perhaps you do not know how much they have spread themselves there, so they cannot quibble that they have got more land than they want, and of course the Upper Quarry, although maybe no use to them, is most certainly no use to us, as it is completely cut off from the road and railway."

He need not have worried, for after a concrete roof collapsed in 1942, burying some 8,000 tons of bombs, the Air Ministry requisitioned even more of the derelict land, for which the taxpayer continued to pay rent to Lord Newborough's estate until 1973.

Bombs were delivered to Glynrhonwy by train, and would later leave the same way, to meet the daily demands of the various squadrons of RAF Bomber Command for their raids on Germany, and also of shipping convoys sailing from Liverpool to supply the RAF and Commonwealth air forces in Africa, the Mediterranean and the Far East.

By the time the war ended many tons of redundant Glynrhonwy high-explosive and incendiary bombs were in a dangerous condition. Some had been buried by accidental rock falls and others were submerged by rainwater in old quarry workings. The RAF's 2MU, specialists in the disposal of explosives, joined 31MU in 1943, and in 1955 Glynrhonwy became a sub-unit of 277MU at RAF Llandwrog (now Caernarfon Airport).

In addition to a wide variety of conventional bombs, Glynrhonwy was used from 1945 to store huge quantities of captured German chemical weapons, including nerve-gas bombs containing Tabun. Shipped from Hamburg to Newport, they were next transported to Glynrhonwy by train, for onward delivery by road to Llandwrog. Originally a training aerodrome, Llandwrog was adapted to dispose of these weapons, some by steaming out the contents into caustic pits, and others by being encased in concrete, for removal by sea from Fort Belan to be dumped north of Ireland and in Beaufort's Dyke, between Scotland and Ulster.[25]

Final clearance of Glynrhonwy began in July 1969, the work being undertaken by the specialised Explosive Ordnance Disposal Flight of 71MU, who were later assisted by the Army's Royal Engineers to speed up the work.

The RAF left both Glynrhonwy and Llandwrog after the work was completed in 1973. The Glynrhonwy site was taken over immediately by the Central Electricity Generating Board, for the big office complex needed during the construction of the pumped-storage hydro-electric generating station deep inside the mountain which was once Dinorwig quarry.

On 4 September 1992 Prime Minister John Major visited Glynrhonwy, much of which had been reclaimed by nature, to inaugurate the new European headquarters and factory of EURO/DPC Ltd, American makers of sophisticated medical diagnostic equipment. One of the factors governing the choice of site was the purity and cleanliness of the air at re-born Glynrhonwy.

John Roberts, Bank Quay

Dissatisfied with Fach-Wen, Greaves and Shelton were on the lookout for something better when Liverpool-born John Roberts, of Bank Quay, Caernarfon, bankrupted himself in 1833, while holding two of Lord Newborough's 21-year slate leases - for Glynrhonwy, at Llanberis, and for Chwarel Llyn Bowydd (Bowydd or Lord's Quarry), at Blaenau Ffestiniog. Born in 1801, Roberts was a pioneer in the transatlantic slate and emigrant trade out of Caernarfon, having bought the brig *Melantho* in 1826, and brig *Belle Isle* in 1827.[26] His ships would return with timber, to add a new commodity to Caernarfon's growing mercantile importance. The *Melantho* was wrecked while laden with slates, in 1831, on the notorious Swellies, always a swirling mass of rock-strewn water just west of Menai suspension bridge. His quarrying leases dated from 1829, when Glynrhonwy appears to have been idle. It was productive by 1831 and remained so until 1834 when Roberts was declared bankrupt with a colossal debt of £30,000, seemingly after draining himself with a costly five-year search for the hidden slate at Blaenau Ffestiniog.[27]

Lord's Quarry

Thus Lord Newborough was looking for a new tenant when J.W. Greaves went to stay with Major Edward W. Mathew (son of Nathaniel Mathew[28]), at Wern, a house near Porthmadog which was later to assume an ever more prominent role in the history of the Greaves family. With an 1834 "take note," or option, in his pocket, Greaves discussed with Mathew the local belief that John Roberts was on the point of success at Blaenau Ffestiniog, and they went to look at the derelict Bowydd. Greaves decided he and Shelton should take it on, and in 1835 they signed 21 year leases for both of John Roberts's abandoned undertakings. That was the year when Greaves also went into a short-lived partnership with Samuel Holland (1803-92), to work an iron and manganese quarry at Llanengan, near Abersoch, in what at first looked like being a profitable enterprise.[29]

Leaving Shelton to look after the Llanberis operations at Fach-Wen and Glynrhonwy, Greaves rented rooms at the Tan-y-bwlch Inn (now the Oakeley Arms), Maentwrog, to concentrate his efforts on the Bowydd and adjoining Foty (Hafoty Cwmbowydd) quarries. Within a year they had decided their future lay in Blaenau Ffestiniog, and in 1836 Shelton and his wife moved into Glan William, an elegant house still standing at Maentwrog, which had been the home of William Edward Oakeley until he moved into Plas Tan-y-bwlch, at the end of 1835. Greaves moved into Tan-yr-allt, Tremadog, in 1838.

When the original Glynrhonwy lease ended in 1856, Greaves renewed it for a further 21 years from 9 August, but the last mention of the venture in his annual accounts was for the year ended 30 September 1862. The site remained idle until he surrendered his lease on 6 June 1873.

The Bonapartes

Little is known about Edwin Shelton, who arrived at Caernarfon some time after 1830 and died in late 1848 or 1849. He retained his Worcestershire home - Thorngrove, at Grimley - while in North Wales, having bought it in 1814 from Prince Lucien Bonaparte, brother of Napoleon. The house is still standing.

Born in Corsica in 1775, Lucien Bonaparte was expelled from Paris in 1804 for insulting his brother by marrying his widowed mistress, a notoriously promiscuous woman, and publicly declaring her a Bonaparte. She had already born him a son, Charles Lucien, in 1803. He went to his brother's Kingdom of Italy where, in 1807, Napoleon offered him the kingdoms of Naples and Spain in return for renouncing his wife. He declined, and accepted instead the Papal title of Prince of Canino. Still under fraternal pressure, Lucien decided to leave Napoleon's sphere of influ-

Greaves's Wharf, Porthmadog, in 1896, the nearer vessel being the locally-built brig Excelsior. Rolling stock in the foreground includes No.107 of the 1836 wooden lath-sided Ffestiniog Railway slate wagons, and some of the 1857 pattern, made of angle iron. Each type carried 2 tons of dressed slates from any of the 15 quarry systems to which Ffestiniog Railway supplied wagons. One of the wider 3-ton type, introduced in 1869, can be seen on the facing track, in front of J. W. Greaves's 1851 office.

ence in 1810, and sail for America. The Royal Navy intercepted his ship in the Mediterranean and he and his family were taken to England as prisoners. He was allowed to buy Thorngrove (for £9,000), there to live the life of a country squire until Napoleon's abdication and exile to Elba in 1814. Lucien returned to Paris and assisted Napoleon's brief return to power in 1815. Lucien Bonaparte died in 1840. His son Charles Lucien Bonaparte eschewed politics for life as a scientist and he visited Aberglaslyn in 1851/2, seemingly with a passing interest in its mineral potential, but he died in 1857 without any further involvement. Another son, Louis Lucien Bonaparte (1813-91), was born at Thorngrove, and spent most of his life in England.

Slates for Liverpool

Several of Greaves' letters were to Charles Moore, of Rumford Street, Liverpool, starting with one which he dated 21 June, i.e. two days before he actually opened his book:

I am sorry to say I am without a vessel for your cargo, but the slates are all ready to be shipped .... Will a smaller craft do, say about 40 tons, if I cannot get one suitable for your order, which is 56 tons?

We do not know the answer to what appears to have been a hazardous suggestion, but on 30 June he again wrote to Moore:

I have at last succeeded in securing a vessel for your cargo, the Orion, *about 50 tons, but was obliged to give 6d (i.e. 2¹/₂ p per ton) more freight than your limit. It was impossible to get a vessel at 4/- (i.e. 20p) but rather than disappoint you of the cargo I will allow you the difference in invoice. The* Orion *will be ready to sail on Wednesday afternoon (i.e. 2 July) and if the weather is favourable will be in your port at the end of the week. Please to have a vessel ready to receive the cargo.*

This letter imparts a lot of information about the process of transporting a cargo of slates the relatively short distance from Porthmadog to Liverpool.

Given favourable winds the *Orion* would take around 72 hours, anchoring in the river and transferring the cargo to a tender. Greaves' willingness to do some bargaining on the freight charge was reciprocated with an attempt to pay for the slates by barter, as we see from the next letter, dated 2 July:

I had the pleasure of the 30th ultimo, and have received yours of same date with order for a cargo of Carnarvon slate, for which I am obliged and which will be attended to immediately.

It will not answer my purpose to take a cargo of coals in payment for the slates as I am not in the trade and such a cargo would entail a good deal of trouble. In the winter I might clear off a lot of the coals at my quarry but at this season of the year they are useless.

Annexed I have pleasure in sending your invoice for your cargo of slate per Orion, *deducting 6d per ton allowance on freight and 5% discount and commission which latter as I before advised you is all I can allow on Port Madoc slates and which I hope you will consider satisfactory.*

I presume you propose settling for this cargo as usual per 21 days Bill on London.

Slate prices

On 7 July 1851 Greaves sent Moore an amended invoice for the *Orion* cargo, a copy of which is fortuitously preserved in the letter book, giving us our first record of the prices he was charging.

Per slates shipped per Orion *@ Liverpool,*
as per bill of lading.

4,000	countess	20 x 10	@ 85/-	£17
4,000	small do.	18 x 10	@ 65/-	£13
5,000	viscountess	18 x 9	@ 55/-	£13/15/-
15,000	ladies	16 x 8	@ 42/6 ·	£31/17/6d

8,000	*small do.*	*14 x 8*	*@ 23/-*	*£9/4/-*

£84/16/6d

less discount and commission 7%   *£5/18/9d*

£78/17/9d

shipping 50 tons 1 cwt @ 8d   *£1/13/4d*

£80/11/1d

less allowance on freight   *£1/5/-*

The prices given are in shillings per M, or *mil* slates. The Welsh word *mil* meant the same as the Latin *mille,* i.e. 1,000, but the quantity it represented in the slate industry was greater. In 1860 H.P.Manley, Collector of Harbour Dues at the Port of Caernarfon, which included Port Dinorwig, told the Harbour Trustees that slates were sold per "long thousand," which, like herrings, meant 1,060.[30] At Blaenau Ffestiniog, however, William Jones, steward at Llechwedd, recorded in 1879 that M meant 1,200 slates.[31] Both were wrong: the actual total was 1,260, as explained in the 1875 price list of the Rhiwbryfdir Slate Company, signed "Mathew & Son." All the prices were specifically listed as "price per M of 1,200," to which was added a footnote: "As 1 cwt over in every ton, and 60 slates over in every M are given at the time of shipment to cover breakage no abatement or further allowance will be made." Thus a slate dealer's M was 1,200 + 60 for the purchaser, but the slatemakers were required to produce 1,300 for every 1,000 for which they were paid. In the 1970s the figures were changed to give the buyer 1,050 for every 1,000 slates ordered, plus the benefit of a 5% discount to cover breakages in transit. This has since been changed to an exact 1,000, plus a 10% discount; the producer's 1,300 being reduced at the same time to 1,000 - which involved management in an overnight increase of 30% in the production bonus paid to the men

Dressing the ladies

The elegant names listed in Greaves' invoice, and still used to describe the different sized slates, were once encapsulated in a poem attributed to an early 19th century judge:[32]

It has been said, as we all must deplore,
    That Grenville and Pitt have made peers by the score;
But now, 'tis asserted, unless I have blundered,
    There's a man that makes peeresses here by the hundred.
He regards neither Portland, nor Grenville, nor Pitt,
    But creates them at once without patent or writ;
By the stroke of a hammer, without the King's aid,
    A lady, or countess, or duchess is made.
Yet high is the station from which they are sent,
    And all their great titles are got by descent;
And where'er they are seen, in a palace or shop,
    Their rank they preserve and are still at the top.
Yet no merit they claim from their birth or connection,
    But derive their chief worth from their native complexion.
This countess or lady, though crowds may be present,
    Submits to be dressed by the hands of a peasant,
And you'll see when her grace is but once in his clutches,
    With how little respect he will handle a duchess.
And all the best judges prefer, it is said,
    A countess in blue to a duchess in red.[33]

These strange names are said to have been started by General Hugh Warburton (1695-1771), co-owner of the Penrhyn quarries,[34] and father of the first Baroness Penrhyn. The list of ladies' titles was extended gradually, causing many amusing incidents, such as the occasion in 1970 when the young Prince of Wales visited an exhibition at the Grand Hotel ballroom, Llandudno, and was told by a slate dresser that His Royal Highness was about to learn how to dress a countess. The pun earned him a glass of sherry from the Prince.[35]

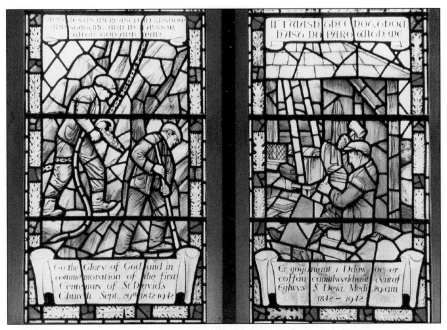

Slate heritage encapsulated in a unique stained glass window in the chancel of Blaenau Ffestiniog parish church. One half shows two men working on the rock face, extracting blocks with pneumatic drill and crowbar; the other half depicts their bargain partner in the mill, splitting the slate, with J.W.Greaves's belt-driven patent dressing engine behind him. The window was installed in 1942 to mark the centenary of the church, and was the gift of Mrs. Rachel Williams-Ellis, granddaughter-in-law of J.W.Greaves.

The full list of names, encompassing slate sizes that are now obsolete, was recorded in the *Caernarvon & Denbigh Herald* on 1 February 1973.[36] Not completely accurate in the *Herald,* the list is amended below to correspond with the measurements used at Blaenau Ffestiniog:

Empresses	26 x 16 inches
Princesses	24 x 14
Duchesses	24 x 12
Small duchesses	22 x 12
Marchionesses	22 x 11

Countesses	20 x 10
Wide countesses	18 x 10
Viscountesses	18 x 9
Ladies	16 x 8
Wide ladies	16 x 10
Small ladies	14 x 8
Queens	variable, to order

Mathew's Quarry

On 2 July 1851 J.W.Greaves sent a note to Nathaniel Mathew's Quarry, across the road at Rhiwbryfdir Middle, *in account with John W.Greaves,* setting out the balance payable on cross trade between the two producers. It would appear that the fancy feminine names for slate sizes were used only when dealing with the general public. The only full comparison between prices charged within the trade and for general sale is for the 16 x 8 inch size, sold to Charles Moore for 42/6d per thousand, and to Mathew for 30/-. Here we see that slabs were sold by weight, at £2/10/- per ton.

Dr (i.e. bought by Mathew)

5 June	*10,000*	*24 x 12*	*@ 115/-*	*£57 - 10 - 00*
7 June	*20,000*	*16 x 8*	*@ 30/-*	*30 - 00 - 00*
23 June	*5,000*	*do*		*7 - 10 - 00*
				£95 - 00 - 00
by discount & commission 8%				*7 - 12 - 00*
				£87 - 8 - 00

Cr (i.e. bought by Greaves)

5 June	*10,000*	*best 22 x 11*	*@ 95/-*	*£47 - 10 - 00*
14 June	*5,000*	*do*		*23 - 15 - 00*

19 June	6,000	24 x 14	@ 157/6	47 - 5 - 00
19 June	150 slabs,	nett 5t 4c	@ 50/-	13 - 0 - 00
				£131 - 10 - 00
to discount & commission 8%				10 - 10 - 6
				£120 - 19 - 6
	by balance			£33 - 11 - 6

The Great Fire of Hamburg

Carl Rindelaub,   12 July 1851
Hamburg.
Dear Sir,
  I much regret it will be quite out of my power to supply the quantity of 24 x 14 and 24 x 12 slates you require on the terms specified - in fact I am quite out of stock of slates. There has been a large fall at the Welsh Slate Company's quarry which has nearly stopped their make of slates, in result of which we have had more orders upon us than we can execute.
  I do not think 100 tons of princesses and duchesses can be obtained from any party here within a reasonable time for this date, but I shall ask anyway Solly and Holland if they can supply such an order.
  I remain, dear sir, yours truly.
P.S. - I tried but Holland has not slates to supply his present orders. Mr Solly has no 24 x 12 or 22 x 11 to spare but could let you have 100 tons of 22 x 12 or 22 x 11. There should be no difficulty in obtaining a vessel on the freight you name.

  This letter is a reminder of the enormous impact made on the North Wales slate industry by the fire which destroyed the heart of the old Hanseatic trading city of Hamburg in May 1842. It was the biggest port in the new German Confederation, and the next most populous city after Berlin, when fire swept through the picturesque centre, which accounted for about a quarter of the city. In 1843 Croydon-born civil engineer William Lindley (1808-1900) was given the task of designing and engineering the rebuilding of the city - he was already on site as engineer-in-chief, 1838-60, for the Hamburg-Bergedorf Railway, and had already given the city a new sewerage system. He turned to Wales for his new roofs, initially to the purple Penrhyn slates shipped from Bangor - prompting Nathaniel Mathew to take himself off to Hamburg with samples of the more pleasing blue-grey Blaenau Ffestiniog product, which immediately found favour with the city's proud free traders. All the Blaenau Ffestiniog slate producers did particularly well out of the Hamburg trade, which lasted for many years - the city's population grew during the 19th century from 130,000 to 700,000. Lindley's restoration work in Hamburg continued until 1865, when he left to become consultant engineer to Frankfurt-on-Main. He retired in 1879 and returned to London, dying in 1900 at 74 Shooter's Hill Road, Blackheath.

Carl Rindelaub, the recipient of this and several ensuing letters and cargoes from Greaves, was a Westphalian, who had migrated to Hamburg in 1831, when he was 30 years of age, and was a well established importer by the time the rebuilding of Hamburg began.[37]

A century later, on four nights between 24 July and 3 August 1943, the Royal Air Force again destroyed Hamburg, inflicting greater destruction than had ever been suffered by so large a city. "The second attack delivered such a concentration of incendiary bombs mixed with high explosive that there arose a fire tornado which raged through the city with a terrifying howl and defied all human counter-measures."[38] By the end of the war RAF Bomber Command had destroyed 55% of the residential area and 60% of the harbour installations, killing 55,000 people. It was ironic that both the 6th (Caernarvonshire & Anglesey) and 7th (Merioneth & Montgomeryshire) Territorial Army Battalions of the Royal Welch Fusiliers should end the war fighting their way into Hamburg, looking in vain for the Welsh slate roofs of which they had heard so much in school and

Taken in 1893 from Llechwedd Barracks, whose ruins can still be seen high above Plas Waenydd (the large house at the entrance to Llechwedd), this photograph shows the Tal Waenydd community in the bottom right. The A470 remains unchanged, traversing the picture through the conifers in the bottom left. The once mighty Oakeley quarry, which closed in 1971, forms the backdrop.

in the folklore of the quarries from whence so many of the volunteers were drawn. The only surviving Llechwedd roof readily identifiable was on the Musikhalle, which was intact - and promptly commandeered by the Forces Broadcasting Unit travelling with the 53rd Division. The Musikhalle was retained for the next nine years as the headquarters of British Forces Network.[39] The victors of the 53rd Welsh Division found a city bereft of anything but the barest needs for human survival, and an enormous British effort was needed to restore administration, health care and basic services.

An 86-ft long (26 metres) wooden ladder being used to examine the natural granite-like roofs which interleave the slate beds at Blaenau Ffestiniog. This photograph was taken in 1893 with the aid of the photographer's magnesium lamps - the inspections were normally done by candlelight!

The Rhiwbryfdir roof falls

Nathaniel N.Solly, named in Greaves' letter to Hamburg, was the agent for the Welsh Slate Company, at their Rhiwbryfdir Lower quarry. He had lived at Bron-y-garth, Porthmadog, before Charles Spooner moved in, c1860. Much later Bron-y-garth became the home of the Cassons, and later Sam V.Beer. Samuel Holland, of Rhiwbryfdir Upper quarry was, as we have seen, an old partner of J.W.Greaves in the abortive Llanengan venture.[40]

"There has been a large fall at the Welsh Slate Company's quarry," wrote Greaves in 1851. This appears to be the earliest record of a series of devastating rock falls affecting both Lord Palmerston's Welsh Slate Company, at Rhiwbryfdir Lower, and Mathew's Rhiwbryfdir Slate Company at Rhiwbryfdir Middle, or Gloddfa Ganol. The Middle quarry was carved out for Nathaniel Mathew by land owner William E.Oakeley, of Plas Tanybwlch, when the leases of Samuel Holland's Upper and Palmerston's Lower came up for renewal in 1839 - each had to give up a portion to create Gloddfa Ganol. Mathew's quarry was vertically above some of the underground working of the Welsh Slate Company, whose greed caused them to start extracting slate from the pillars needed to hold the weight of the mountain above.

For further records of the persistent falls in the holdings across the road to Llechwedd one has to turn to the unpublished diaries of J.W.Greaves's son, John Ernest Greaves, who took over the management of the family business when the founder retired in 1870. The founder died in 1880, and in his diary for that year J.Ernest Greaves wrote, on 27 June: "Great fall at both the Middle and Welsh Slate Company." Again, on 18 July: "Fall at Welsh Slate Company." On 6 December 1882 the manager of the Welsh Slate Company wrote: "The long expected disasters have at last come upon us and all the quarry is today at a stand." [41]

On 22 January 1883 Edward Mathew was a lunch guest of J.E.Greaves at Plas Weunydd,[42] the house built by J.W.Greaves in 1870, at the entrance to Llechwedd, and now accommodating the offices of J.W.Greaves

& Sons. They talked at length about the serious situation across the road, where the Mathew family had not only seen the collapse of their best slate beds into the Welsh Slate Company's underground chaos, but had lost their lease on the site in 1877, when Oakeley decided he would himself work both the Middle and Upper quarries - the Welsh Slate Company had earlier negotiated a new lease, so that their Lower quarry was not absorbed into the Oakeley operation until forced out of business in 1883. On 16 February 1883 J.E.Greaves noted: "Great fall at Welsh Slate Company's quarry at 8 am." It was calculated that 6½ million tons of rock had collapsed into the workings, thus ending for ever the Welsh Slate Company's boast of being "the biggest slate mine in the world" - killed off by remote control avarice in London and local inefficiency. On 10 June 1883 Greaves recorded yet another fall at Oakeley's Middle, or Gloddfa Ganol quarry, whose safety had always depended on the stability of the bigger underground workings of the Welsh Slate Company. These two collapses resulted in famous litigation and the Welsh Slate Company's being ordered to pay the colossal sum of £110,000 to the Oakeley Slate Company. (Prime Minister Lord Palmerston, chairman of the Welsh Slate Company, had died in 1865). Underground restrictions imposed by H.M. Inspector of Mines & Quarries within parts of the Oakeley complex, the limited availability of open cast slate, the inability to find a buyer (Llechwedd having declined the option to buy it for £7,000), led to its closure in 1971. A small section of the former Oakeley quarry was reopened in 1974 for some surface working of the slate and underground visits for walking tourists - a lesser reflection of the more sophisticated operation pioneered in 1972 by Llechwedd Slate Caverns, who have since won every major tourism award.

Yesterday and tomorrow, but ...

Mr Jonathan Reynolds,   *3 July 1851*
Merthyr Tydfil.

    I am obliged for your favour enquiring prices and particulars of my Festiniog slates, with a view to engaging in the trade, but in reply I beg to inform you that I am in the habit of supplying Messrs Watson & Richards, of Cardiff, as also a gentleman in your own town. I am not desirous of extending my connection further in that neighbourhood.

Yours faithfully,

John W.Greaves

F.Winther,   *4 August 1852*
Copenhagen.

    I beg to inform you that I have so great a demand for slates from my old customers that I should disappoint them were I to accept orders from any fresh applicants, and therefore I am not in a position at present to supply you, but I am opening up some new quarries from which I shall have a large quantity of slates and if you think proper to write to me again next summer I hope I shall then be able to supply you.

Mr Winther did come back, and Llechwedd slates can now be found on numerous Danish buildings, notably on the State Railway, Copenhagen Town Hall, various army barracks, customs houses, hospitals and schools.

Explosives

J.S.Spooner,   *16 December 1852*
Bryn Llewelyn,
Festiniog.

Dear Spooner,

    I think you should have informed me you had raised the price of powder. I can only give you the preference so long as you sell at the same price

Miners driving the initial channel for the start of a new chamber, which would be developed over ten or more years as the slate was extracted. The miner below is wearing the famous trwsus Ffestin, virtually the uniform of his trade. The name was a locally corrupted version of trwsus ffystyn, or "fustian trousers." Fustian was a thick off-white cotton material, of a particular weave developed in ancient times at Al-Fustat, the original Cairo. .

as others. When Mr Curtis was here lately I promised to try his powder and I send you his invoice. As you offered to supply me at 40/- less 2½% that should be acted on till you informed me to the contrary. I send you a cheque for £39 but if it is not satisfactory I will send you the £2.

Virtually nothing has been written about the explosives used to extract the slate at Blaenau Ffestiniog. Gunpowder was invented in 1250, and until 1854 was the sole blasting agent used in slate quarrying. Ffestiniog's first supplies of gunpowder came during the 18th century from Bala, which was the principal market town for the community then centred on the older community of Llan Ffestiniog. The community's 1795 population of 60 accommodated three taverns: Ty Isa (later Newborough Arms), Ty Ucha (later the Eagles Inn) and Yr Efail (Pengwern Arms).[43] Only two residents could speak English when Cumberland-born Thomas Casson and his wife Esther took the licence of Ty Ucha in 1800.[44] Bala was used both for buying general supplies and for selling the community's main product: stockings produced by the women as soon as a girl was old enough to manipulate a set of knitting needles. The gunpowder from Bala always came in 6 lb bags.[45] By the end of the century powder could be bought from Ffestiniog grocer David Lloyd, who was still supplying Bowydd (or Lord's quarry) in the 1820s.[46]

M.J.T. Lewis notes that a building shown on Tyddyn Isa quay, on the River Dwyryd, in Brunel's 1845 plan for the proposed Worcester to Porthdinllaen railway (to capture the Irish Mail contract), is also shown in the 25-inch Ordnance Survey of 1887, where it is identified as a magazine. The 21-ft square building is still standing, and appears to have been purpose built, for it has no windows. In addition to the Tyddyn Isa magazine, which would have been supplied by small boats coming up river from the estuary, there was a magazine on Ynys Tywyn, Porthmadog, by 1845.

Curtis & Harvey powder

The Curtis & Harvey magazines beside the Ffestiniog Railway's Boston Lodge works were not built until 1865, but Greaves' letter shows Charles B.Curtis (1795-1876) already active in the area at least as early as 1852. The firm was founded in 1820 by banker Sir William Curtis, MP, a former Lord Mayor of London. The first partners were his son Charles Curtis and friend W.G.Harvey, who already had an ancient powder factory at Hounslow. The name Curtis & Harvey was retained for a new limited company registered in 1898, later absorbed by Nobel's Explosives Company, which became part of ICI.

Presumably both James Swinton Spooner and Curtis & Harvey had separate powder magazines in the area, from which to supply the 1852 needs of J.W.Greaves and other quarry owners, but where were they? J.S.Spooner, of Bryn Llewelyn,[47] was the civil engineer son of James Spooner, of Morfa Lodge, Porthmadog, surveyor and secretary to Ffestiniog Railway. From whence did he obtain his supplies in sufficient quantity to challenge Curtis & Harvey? Was there already a gunpowder factory at Penrhyndeudraeth by 1852?

Cooke's Explosives Ltd.

The Penrhyndeudraeth factory now in the process of decommissioning was first licensed to make explosives in 1876, but when R.T.Cooke set up Cooke's Explosives Ltd, in 1922, he believed the site had been used for a similar purpose since about 1845,[48] probably for gunpowder though guncotton, based on nitrate of cellulose, was discovered in 1845. Around 1887 the French chemist Favier offered his patent for the nitro-glycerine based *explosifs Favier* to Sir George Elliott, MP, of Durham, chairman of several colliery companies. The powder gave off less heat and fumes than gunpowder and was more powerful. In 1888 Elliott founded Miners' Safety

Explosive Ltd, in Essex, to make what became known in this country as ammonite. In 1916 R.T.Cooke bought the controlling interest in ammonite from Elliott's trustees and moved production to Penrhyndeudraeth in 1924, on a site he had already acquired adjoining Cooke's acid and nitro-glycerine factory. This arrangement put at the disposal of the ammonite factory a plentiful supply of the strong nitric acid required for the manufacture of TNT and tri-nitro-napthalene, which ingredients are used in ammonite.

Cooke's original conception was to provide a self-contained independent factory for making and supplying blasting explosives and assembling detonators. Raw materials were delivered by sea to Porthmadog, in the MV *Florence Cooke*.[49] Nitrate of soda came direct from Chile, and was used at Penrhyndeudraeth to make nitric acid, which was processed to give up its nitrogen and oxygen to glycerine, for incorporation in Penrhyn Powder and gelignite.

The Penrhyndeudraeth site was chosen for its ample supply of water, natural protection afforded by two ranges of rock which divided the factory into three distinct areas, and natural difference in levels for gravitation of the nitro-glycerine for washing. Though retaining the name of Cooke's Works, the factory was part of ICI's Nobel's Explosives Company in 1994, when it was announced that manufacture would end early in 1995. No gunpowder was ever made by Cooke's at Penrhyndeudraeth.

The Cwm-y-glo explosion

Earlier entrepreneurs introduced nitro-glycerine to North Wales in its highly unstable liquid form. Although black powder remains the preferred explosive in the slate industry, because it does least damage to the rock, there are times when harder unwanted stone needs a more powerful explosive. In 1846 Ascanio Sobrero discovered nitro-glycerine, a volatile oil that could be detonated by a relatively minor shock, its fragility increasing with heat. Alfred Nobel invented the safer nitro-glycerine-based mixture he called dynamite in 1862, but continued to make his hazardous "blasting oil" near Hamburg.

Five containers, each containing a ton of the Hamburg liquid, were unloaded at Caernarfon in 1869. That there was a ready market for the liquid is proved by the prompt despatch, in two horse-drawn carts, of two tons of it, encased in straw, intended for the Llanberis magazine of Webb & Co.[50] The carts were left standing in the June sun while the carters refreshed themselves at each of the two public houses in Cwm-y-glo. The explosive oil, slowly cooking in its straw oven, would have been very unstable by the time the carts resumed their journey, and soon after they left the village there was a devastating explosion. All that remained of the carts was a wheel and some harness, found half-a-mile away, 400 feet up the slopes of Cefn Du.[51] As well as the two drivers, three other people were killed (including a quarryman on his way home from Glynrhonwy) and eight were seriously injured. If the explosion had happened ten minutes earlier Cwm-y-glo would have been destroyed. Seared into the local folk memory as *ffrwydriad a powdwr-oel* (i.e. "the nitro-glycerine explosion"), the Cwm-y-glo accident resulted in an immediate ban (albeit temporary) on the importation of the substance, and a prompt change in the law governing its transportation. That ended the use of liquid nitro-glycerine in the Welsh slate industry.

Giving him the oil

When Sir O.M.Edwards, founder of the best-known dynasty in the Welsh Establishment,[52] visited Llechwedd slate mines in 1893 he was bemused by an unfamiliar Welsh idiom, *rhoi'r oel am byth,* used by strikers to explain the cause of their dispute, i.e. "giving him the oil for ever."[53] Having asked what it meant, O.M. was told it was the local way of saying a stubborn man had been sent away to be made more flexible.

The idiom has long passed out of usage but in the late 1940s it was familiar to Llanrug newspaper columnist Glan Rhythallt, i.e. Isaac Lloyd (1875-1959), who told the author, during one of his weekly visits to the Herald Office, in Caernarfon's Castle Square, that it meant giving a final farewell to someone you did not wish to see again. It was an allusion to the nitro-glycerine explosion, a macabre example of the black humour of the slate quarrymen of North Wales.

J.W.Greaves had abandoned his Glynrhonwy quarry at the end of 1862, offering anyone interested alternative work at Llechwedd, where there was a shortage of labour. Men had been transferring between the two quarries ever since 1846, and as labour conditions were regarded as superior at Blaenau Ffestiniog some of those made redundant at Glynrhonwy in 1862 would have either moved permanently or would have commuted weekly, using the barracks available to them on the Cribau slopes at Llechwedd.

When O.M.Edwards first heard the idiom "giving him the oil" it seemed very localised, possibly a Llechwedd expression, suggesting it may have been imported by Llanberis men who, by 1893, had died or retired, so that those to whom O.M. spoke would not know its origins. There is no longer any trace of the idiom in Blaenau Ffestiniog or Llanberis.

Gunpowder

A description of how explosives were imported at Porthmadog in 1839 has been preserved.[54] The ship was not allowed to enter the harbour but discharged the gunpowder into a wooden barge, which flew a red flag when bringing small transhipments to the Ffestiniog Railway terminus. There it was transferred into specially constructed powder wagons, whose sheet iron side plates had been wrapped over the top to form a roof. The railway's own regulations stipulated that powder wagons were to be kept as far as possible from the locomotive while being hauled from the harbour to Curtis & Harvey's three magazines at Boston Lodge. Similar powder wagons were introduced by the railway's customers for the conveyance of black powder from the Curtis & Harvey magazines to the individual quarry stores. One such wagon is included in the collection of old narrow gauge rolling stock now on public display at Llechwedd Slate Caverns.

Greaves' letter to Spooner refers to a price of 40/- per cwt, which was £40 per ton, on which there was £1 discount. On 10 January 1853 he again wrote to Spooner, this time ostensibly from Tan-yr-allt, his home at Tremadog, though the letter formed part of the same book at the Porthmadog office:

Dear Spooner,

I am glad to hear from Holland that you continue the price of powder at £40. I have desired my man to apply to you for the next ton he requires. That we may have a clear understanding of the price in the future I will, if you please, take all I require for the next twelve months from you at £40 per ton, less 2½% for cash, the quality to be equal to your present FOF.[55] My consumption is about one ton a month.

Samuel Holland, across the road, at Rhiwbryfdir Upper quarry, appears to have been less than accurate in his discussions with Greaves, for Spooner was unwilling to sell his powder at £40 a ton, as we see from the next letter, dated 10 March 1853:

When you have a stock of FOF will you supply me with all I require of this quality for the next twelve months at 42/- less 2½%, say 12 tons. If so I will take it, payment as usual, cash on delivery. I have an offer on these terms from a neighbour.

This effusive letter, signed by Greaves himself, suggests Spooner's price was better than anything Curtis & Harvey could offer - despite the bluff of a neighbour's supposed offer of £42 a ton. That points to Spooner's having the commercial advantage of access to a nearby manufacturer. Did that mean Penrhyndeudraeth? In a period of economic stability, with no big war in progress to push up the demand for gunpowder, there was rapid inflation in the price, as we see from a letter which Greaves wrote to

J. W. Greaves's first slabbing mill of 1852, showing the slate sawing table invented by Greaves in 1850, though not patented.

Spooner on 15 April 1853. In the space of four months the price of gunpowder at Blaenau Ffestiniog had soared by an alarming 10%, from £2 per hundredweight to £2.20p:

> *You may book my order for 12 tons of powder FOF of equal quality to that I have hitherto had, at 44/-, subject to a discount of $2^{1}/_{2}\%$.*

Slate slabs

Messrs Checketts & Buffry,   *11 July 1851*
Emscote.[56]

> *I regret I have only about 20 tons of draining slates and I have not yet made my mill to make slabs, and my neighbours have so many orders for them that they cannot supply me with the quantity you require.*

This and subsequent letters on the subject to different customers, plot the history of Greaves' first slabbing mill, now a museum exhibit which visitors to Llechwedd Slate Caverns see when they alight at the end of their return journey on the Miners' Tramway. Construction of the mill appears to have commenced on Monday, 3 May 1852 but it was not in full production until late April 1853. Such a long delay requires some explanation, for the letters demonstrate some small degree of production from August 1852, suggesting the structure of the Floor 2 Mill was then complete, and that the equipment was in place. The problem lay in the inefficiency of the sawing and planing equipment, not because of inherent design faults, but probably because of the difficulty in linking it to J.W.Greaves's natural source of power, in the two Barlwyd lakes (Llynnau Barlwyd), above Llechwedd. These lakes were harnessed to enormous water wheels, the first of which was installed beside the Floor 2 Mill, at the northern gable end. The overhead drive shaft from this wheel is still in situ, complete with pulley wheels cast by J.Dunnell Garrett & Co Ltd, of Ffestiniog.

J.W.Greaves invented the first successful slate sawing table in 1850 but did not patent it.[57] "This proved to be a perfect success and is used with a few slight alterations in most of the quarries."[58] The three specimens now on public display are Greaves' original (at the northern end of the mill), the near identical design made and patented by G.Owens, at the Union Iron Works, Porthmadog, and the variation patented in 1888 by the De Winton works at Caernarfon. They all used a steel circular saw, which had to be removed for sharpening and re-setting every four hours.

Also displayed in the mill are two of the Greaves' patent slate dressing engines, one made by William Lewis, at the Ffestiniog Foundry, Tanygrisiau, and the other by R.Jones & Sons, Porthmadog. These machines are known universally as Greaves' patent, and also date from 1850 though redesigned and re-patented in 1886 by J.W.Greaves's son Richard.

L.M.Tatham   *10 March 1852*
I have engaged a vessel of 28 tons to take the cargo of slates ordered by Mr Heritage to Chester, at 6/- per ton, and she will be loaded tomorrow. I am not in a position to take orders for slabs as my mill is not built.

Richard Cail,   *7 May 1852*
Newcastle on Tyne
  I have this week begun to build my mill for sawing and as soon as I am in a position to supply slabs I will not fail to write to you.

C.H. Hawkins,   *4 August 1852*
Colchester.
  I regret I cannot send any slabs. I cannot make them as my sawing mill is not finished and I cannot get them from my neighbours as they have not enough for the supply of their customers. The Edith *waits a fair wind. I have ordered for the cargo to be insured.*

C.H. Hawkins,   *12 August 1852*
  The Edith *sailed last evening. The four slabs we could make were put in her.*

Edward Sibbering   *17 September 1852*
  I have no slabs at present. I am now building a mill to make them but it will not be complete for some months.

C.H. Hawkins   *23 October 1852*
  The slabs shall be sent with the next cargo

John Stephens,   *2 March 1853*
Worcester Wharf, Birmingham.
  I have not yet finished my mill for making squares. As soon as I have done so and have some squares ready I will write to you and I hope to send you the first sample.

William Dawber & Sons,   *18 March 1853*
Hull
  The Welsh Slate Company will supply you with the slab you require - planed one side and about 1/4 *inch thick.*

Richard Cail   26 April 1853
    I will be ready to ship for you this week and as many of the slabs I can prepare for you before the cargo is loaded.

Shipbuilding

C.H.Hawkins,   23 July 1851
Colchester.
    I have arranged with Mr Solly for him to ship for you 150 tons of Princesses, all of which I expect to be ready in the course of the following week.
    I am glad to hear we are to have the pleasure of seeing you here, where I have no doubt satisfactory arrangements can be made for the supply of the rest of the slates.
    A shipbuilder at Pwllheli is, I hear, beginning a vessel of 1,000 tons. I shall be happy to introduce you to him, if you think it probable you can supply him with timber.

    Greaves appears to have been misinformed. The 659 ton *William Carey*[59] had been launched at Pwllheli three years earlier, being the largest merchant ship built in Wales up to that time. A full-rigged ship, she was built at the yard of William Jones (1793-1855), of Brynhyfryd, a prominent Baptist - hence the name of William Carey (1761-1834), founder of the Baptist Missionary Society, and not William Carey (1769-1846) who was Bishop of St Asaph 1830-46. William Jones owned 56/64ths of the ship and his son Griffith owned the remainder. The next vessel of comparable size, the 693 ton barque *Margaret Pugh*,[60] did not emerge from Pwllheli until 1862.

C.H.Hawkins,   4 August 1852
    I cannot induce anyone here to give an order for oak timber. It appears to be a drag here, a considerable quantity has been consigned here from Southampton and is being sold at a very low price.

C.H.Hawkins,   *12 August 1852*
Colchester.

     I wish I could send you an order for oak timber but there has been only one vessel begun here recently, and that a small one by Henry Jones, and he is overstocked with timber.

One cannot deduce the vessel to which Greaves was referring in this letter. Henry Jones had launched the 59 ton smack *Onyx*[61] in 1851. Greaves could not have been referring to the substantial vessel described below in his letter to Chapman & Son, on 4 May 1852. Henry Jones was the first shipbuilder to establish himself within the new harbour at Porthmadog, in 1824.[62] By 1856 there were six flourishing shipbuilders at Porthmadog and between them they perfected the merchant schooner design to earn an international reputation. Henry Jones completed 54 vessels before relinquishing his Canol-y-clwt yard in 1860 for incorporation in the neighbouring quay of J.W.Greaves. His biggest vessel was the 353 ton barque *Henry Jones,*[63] built for Liverpool owners in 1850. The year before he had built the barque *Ann Melhuish,* 347 tons[64] and in 1843 the brig *Mary Holland,* 341 tons.[65]

Carl Rindelaub,   *24 April 1853*
Hamburg.

     I have spoken to our shipbuilders respecting the oak timber. They say it will not answer for our ships, which are all A1 for 12 years, and that if built with Hamburg oak they would only class A1 for nine years. Do you know if this is so?

The shipbuilders of Porthmadog and Pwllheli used local oak from Ardudwy, in Merioneth, and other timbers imported from Canada.[66] Cash flow was the biggest problem affecting local shipbuilders, as explained in the following letter:

"Please to employ experienced men to stow," wrote J. W. Greaves to his Liverpool agent for a cargo being transhipped to Australia. This photograph of 1893 shows the techniques used at Greaves' Wharf, Porthmadog. Bundles of slate were slid down planks into the ship, where packers stood by with specially shaped mallets to wedge the cargo tight with straw.

Messrs Chapman & Son,   *4 May 1852*
Chepstow.

In reply to your enquiry, I consider Henry Jones is quite safe for any amount you may have trusted him. He has a very considerable property in shipping but is always short of money, in consequence of overbuilding himself - he has today launched a vessel that will carry about 350 tons, and I believe she is all his own. I would advise you to render the bill and rest assured it will be paid.

This refers to the launch of the 238 ton brig *North Wales,* whose first master was R.Pritchard. While reassuring Chapman & Son about the status of Henry Jones, Greaves presumably did not know he needed to be wary of his inquirer, but while visiting Chepstow on 6 April 1871 the company's salesman noted in his diary: "Chapman & Sons gone to the bad long ago."[67]

All at sea

Most members of the Greaves family had vessels named after them by the Porthmadog shipbuilders, the person named often performing the launching ceremony. By a bizarre coincidence each of these ships met with a disastrous end.

J.W.GREAVES: brig, 220 tons, 1868, named after the founder of Llechwedd. Lost off Imbituba, the southern Brazil coal port, 1881; salvaged and renamed the *Prima de Janeiro.*

EDITH: schooner, 87 tons, 1851. Named after a daughter of J.W.Greaves, who was part-owner. Lost with all hands off Kinsale, southern Ireland, 1875.

CONSTANCE: schooner, 142 tons, 1862, named after a daughter of J.W.Greaves, who married, in 1874, Lt-General Sir Henry Smyth (uncle of Robert Baden-Powell). Sank after a collision off St Catherine's Point, Isle of Wight, 1890.

MABEL: schooner, 56 tons, 1864, named after Ellen Mabel Greaves, daughter of J.W.Greaves, who married, in 1877, the Rev John Clough Williams-Ellis. Wrecked at Safi, the port of Marrakesh, Morocco, 1892.

BLANCHE CURRIE: barquentine, 193 tons, 1875, named after a sister of Sir Osmond Williams. (see *EVELYN,* below). Lost with all hands off Cape Race, Newfoundland, 1914.

A busy scene at Greaves' Wharf, Porthmadog, c1909. The two-masted schooner on the left is the 104-ton Edith Eleanor, *built in 1881. Next is the 186-ton barquentine* C. E. Spooner, *built in 1878 and sold to Portugal in 1912 (when she was renamed* Senhora de Monte). *In front of it is the wooden paddle steamer* Wave of Life, *delivered as the port's first tugboat in 1862. On the right is the 126-ton three-masted schooner* Elizabeth Pritchard, *built in 1909 and sold to Newfoundland in 1916. The model in a bottle (below) is something of a mystery. Owned by Sir Osmond Williams, it carries the name* Wern *on its pennant, but the only* Wern *known to the family was registered as a brigantine.*

EDWARD SEYMOUR: barquentine, 172 tons, 1876, named after Edward Seymour Greaves, son of J.W.Greaves. Wrecked on southern point of Ile d'Anticosti, in the Gulf of Labrador. Canada, 1902.

ELLEN GREAVES: brig, 254 tons, 1876, see *MABEL*, above. Wrecked on Aruba Island, north of Venezuela, 1897.

WERN: brigantine, 174 tons, 1876. Named after the home of R.M.Greaves. Lost in collision with a pilot steamer off Point Lynas, Anglesey, 1906.

EVELYN: brig, 202 tons, 1877, named after Frances Evelyn Greaves, daughter of J.W.Greaves, who was married in 1880 to (Sir) Osmond Williams, the first baronet. Abandoned in the Atlantic, May 1914.

HILDA: barquentine, 185 tons, 1877, named after a daughter of J.W.Greaves, who remained unmarried. Wrecked on the island of Buen Ayre (also known as Bonaire), east of Curaçao, West Indies, 1883.

MARIANNE GREAVES: brig, 185 tons, 1877, named after the wife of J.Ernest Greaves (son of J.W,Greaves). Lost in the Atlantic 1890.

RICHARD GREAVES: schooner, 118 tons, 1885, named after Richard Methuen Greaves, son of J.W.Greaves. Abandoned in the Atlantic, 1908.

DOROTHY: schooner, 142 tons, 1891, named after a daughter of J.Ernest Greaves, who had a quarter share in the vessel, his brother R.M.Greaves also having a quarter. Lost in a collision off Cape Trafalgar, southern Spain, in 1905.

The good ship Edith

C.H.Hawkins,   *11 September 1851*

I have now the pleasure of sending your invoice for slates shipped according to your order on the good ship Edith. *I have ordered the cargo insured and as soon as I learn the charge I will draw upon you. The* Edith *will sail either the morrow or on Saturday. She has 2/4 [sic] tons of spars for Mr W.Hawkins. I hope to arrange the accounts for building the* Edith *tomorrow. I think you will be pleased with her. I believe there has been no vessel better built at Port Madoc.*

C.H.Hawkins,   *15 September 1851*

I enclose a copy of the insurance of the cargo per Edith. *You will notice the low rate charged - should you have occasion to insure I think you could get it done through Jones & Price at a lower rate than by any other persons.*

Hugh Roberts will show you the account of particulars of the cost of the Edith. *The total is £1,540/8/1d, which includes ship's stores (victuals, etc), port charges, insurance and all expenses. Your 4/16th costs £385/2/0 towards which you have paid £98, leaving £287/2/0 still due, which you will please to pay to my account with Greenway & Greaves, Bankers, Warwick, together with £143/11/0 due from Mr Martin, which you will be so kind as to receive from him.*

The *Edith* was built at the yard of William Jones for J.W.Greaves & Co, in which C.H.Hawkins, of Colchester, had a quarter share, and the Martin named in the letter owned 3/32nds. These letters refer to her maiden voyage. Her first master, Captain Hugh Roberts, had worked for Greaves since 1849, initially as master of the *Independence*,[68] a schooner built at New Brunswick in the 1830s and bought by Greaves in 1841. Hugh Roberts survived the ship's loss in 1875 and continued to serve the Greaves family for many years. He was the first master of the schooner *Constance* on which three of his sons learnt their seamanship.[69]

Not so Swift

George Sibbering   *15 November 1852*
In reply to yours of the 12th, the Swift *sailed from here the 20th ultimo, but was driven back by contrary winds on the 23rd. She sailed again the last week in October. I trust you have heard something ere this, as I find in Saturday's* List [13 November] *the following: "The* Swift, *Davies, arrived at Bristol (Nov 12) from Cardiff." But I cannot reconcile this with your letter at all. I shall be happy to hear of the vessel's safe arrival.*

The Independence

Captain Hugh Roberts,   *3 July 1851*
Independence.
     I send you enclosed order on the Union Bank, Liverpool, £100 - which I hope you will receive safely. Mr Greaves wishes you to bring home with you for the quarry 24 yards of ¼ inch chain, at the price named in your letter. Acknowledge receipt of the money by return of post.

Carl Rindelaub,
Hamburg.
17 September 1852
     I am glad to hear the Independence *delivered her cargo to your satisfaction but I regret I cannot now send you another cargo from Caernarvon as I have no slates on hand there and am making but very few, and I have now raised the price of them to the same as the Port*

Captain Hugh Roberts, of Porthmadog, with his bride, during their honeymoon in Antwerp.

Madoc slates. I can, if you please, send you a cargo of 22 x 11 and 18 x 9 from here, but I have no 18 x 10 or 16 x 10. I understand from your letter dated May 19 that you wished the princesses for Lubeck from here and I have made all I could of them for you, and have now 20,000 ready, which I shall be happy to ship to Hamburg, making up the cargo with 22 x 11 and 18 x 9.

I thank you for sending the boots, for which I suppose the captain paid.

Captain Thomas Parry ,   *25 September 1852*
Independence.

As soon as you arrive at Newcastle please to drop me a line as you are to leave the Independence *and come here to join the* Rose *with the least possible delay. I will send a man to take charge of your vessel and you must remain at Newcastle until he arrives. The £25 came safe to hand.*

Please to bring with you the boots you bought for me at Hamburg.

Captain Thomas Parry,   *4 October 1852*
Independence.

I am glad that you have arrived safe at Newcastle. William Humphreys leaves here today by Mail and as soon as he arrives you are to leave the vessel in his charge and come home without delay. Please to pay the men and make up your accounts to the day you leave so as to close your account entirely for the Independence.

Remember the boots from Hamburg.

Thomas Hughes,   *29 October 1852*
Chemist etc,
Pwllheli.

The Independence, *Captain Mr Humphreys, is coming from Plymouth with a cargo of limestones. Would you like to have them? And you would oblige me by sending the enclosed note to the captain as soon as the vessel arrives inside the Gimblet.*[70]

Captain William Humphreys,   *29 October 1852*
Independence.
    I have written to Thomas Hughes, chemist, asking him to take the
limestones. They are worth 3/- a ton here, and unless you can do better bring
them on here.

A windbound Rose

Mr John Prichard,   *5 October 1852*
56 Parliament Street,
Liverpool.
    In answer to your letter of the 29th ultimo, I have to inform you that
I do not require a master for the schooner Rose *as I have already engaged one.*

The *Rose* was a 92-ton schooner built in Nova Scotia in 1846. She first
sailed from Greaves' Wharf on 22 June 1849, carrying 156 tons of slates
for Lubeck, under Captain William Humphreys. J.W.Greaves' ledger contains the following entry for 1 October 1849: "*Rose* schooner, to balance
£924; Shield Brothers, Dr £671, Cr £500; Insurance Society, £15/18/
9d." Frederick Shield & Co, of Newcastle-upon-Tyne, were among
Greaves's first customers, and were persuaded to become a shareholder in
his *Rose*.

Ball & Co,   *25 October 1852*
Bristol.
    On receipt of yours for Sunderland I engaged the Rose *at 9/- per ton*
freight to take about 60 tons to Sunderland and the rest of the cargo to New-
castle.

Three days later Greaves wrote to *Jones & Price, of 3 Church Street, Clements*
Lane, London:

Please to insure 80 tons 18 cwt of slates from hence to Newcastle-on-Tyne, shipped per the Rose, *Thomas Parry, master, value £121.*

Richard Cail, Esq.,   *29 October 1852*
Newcastle-on-Tyne.
          The master of the Bertholly *found his vessel required some repairs .... I engaged the* Rose. *I expect she will sail tomorrow.*

Richard Cail,   *10 November 1852*
          The Rose *has not yet sailed but I expect she will get out tomorrow.*

Richard Cail   *12 November 1852*
          I am quite out of stock of slates and have a stem for all sizes.   The Rose *is still here.*

Ball & Co.   *22 November 1852*
Bristol.
          The Rose *sailed from here last Monday, November 15th. I have just received a note from the master, dated Milford, November 19, where he shelters.*

Richard Cail.   *22 December 1852*
          Thinking that you feel anxious about the Rose *before this time I beg to advise you that she and many other vessels that sailed from here at the same time are still windbound at Milford.*

G. Waters,   *5 January 1853*
Chepstow.
          The Independence *is still here, windbound. There are about 40 vessels loaded, waiting for a fair wind.*

Richard Cail.   *10 January 1853*
          I reply to your enquiry. I am happy to inform you the Rose *is safe at Milford, windbound.*

Gone with the wind

Ingram & Clarke,   *16 October 1852*
Liverpool.
Please inform me when you have done respecting the slates sent as joint account to San Francisco.

This is the first evidence of an export of Llechwedd slates to the American continent. California, on the Pacific seaboard, was under Mexican domination until 1847, when the United States army seized it. A year later it was ceded to the USA. Gold was discovered in 1849, and in 1850 California was admitted to the Union. Greaves was in at the very start of the conversion of Yerba Buena into the newly named settlement of San Francisco, and he roofed many of the elegant buildings destroyed in the famous earthquake of 1868 - any surviving Llechwedd roofs being lost in the 1872 earthquake. There being no Panama Canal until 1914, the small sailing ships conveying the slates from Porthmadog had to negotiate the empty vastness of both the North and South Atlantic, the storms of Cape Horn, and the emptiness of the Pacific to reach San Francisco - where there was nothing better than unprofitable ballast for the start of the return trip.

Welsh slatemen of America

Blaenau Ffestiniog was instrumental in establishing the American slate industry which, by the beginning of this century, was landing its products at Liverpool at less than the cost of its Welsh rivals.

America's first slate beds were found in 1734, and opened up commercially in 1785, largely by Welshmen, at Peach Bottom, on the Pennsylvania/Maryland state line - where a less than accurate commemorative plaque has been erected.[71] Brothers William and James Reese left North Wales

The Argentine National Bank, Buenos Aires, one of the countless prestigious buildings across the world roofed with J. W. Greaves's slates from Llechwedd Slate Mines.

in 1725 and took a plot of land from the British colonial government, near the Susquehanna river, in York County, Pennsylvania. While excavating rock for new farm buildings in 1734 or 1735 they found the slate which they immediately recognised. Furthermore they knew enough about the Welsh craft to make themselves the first slate roof on the American continent.

Virginia provided the second American slate quarry, opened in 1787 to roof the new state capitol at Richmond, to whence the administration had moved seven years earlier from Williamsburg where, in 1776, the Continental Congress had unanimously adopted its historic resolution that the United Colonies ought to be free and independent states. Thomas Jefferson's Declaration of Independence was read soon afterwards in the Williamsburg Courthouse, bearing the signatures of 56 colonial representatives, of whom 11 for certain, including Jefferson, and possibly as many as 17, were of Welsh descent.

The American slate industry was set up in a geological arc stretching from North Blanchard, in Maine, through the states of Vermont, New York, Pennsylvania and Maryland, to Arvonia, in Virginia - an area in which one can still hear the Welsh language spoken, although the quarries have passed into history - including the Welsh Slate Company, Vermont, founded c1860 by Hugh Rowlands, of Llechwedd.

In 1993 descendants of the pioneering Reese brothers and of 60 Ffestiniog families who emigrated to Fairhaven, Vermont, between 1841 and 1860, visited Llechwedd Slate Caverns.

Benjamin Hewetson

Mr B.Hewetson,   *14 July 1851*
King's Lynn.
 I can engage a vessel of the size you require at 8/6d per ton freight (she is A1). My ladies are 16 x 8, for which I charge 37/6d per M. I have 15 to 20 M of 16 x 9 best, for which I charge 42/6d. My inferiors are very good, both straight and even in surface.

B.Hewetson, Esq.   *4 July 1851*
 I have pleasure in handing you the enclosed cheque for your 1/16th share in the Benjamin Hewetson, *5th dividend, amount £6/16/10d, which I hope you will receive safely. When I lately took the management of the ship's accounts I found them so much neglected by my predecessor and consequently confided that I am obliged to wait the return of Captain Lloyd before I can make out a correct statement. Capt Lloyd, however, expects to be here in the course of 6 or 7 weeks and you may depend upon receiving the statement as soon after his return as possible.*
       W.C.Young, ship's husband

Benjamin Hewetson   *20 October 1852*
    I have engaged the Bertholly, *90 tons, but as the freights are rising and the vessels scarce I have been obliged to give 10/-.*

A page in J.W.Greaves' ledger book contains the entry: "1 October 1849, *Benjamin Hewetson,* schooner, to balance £120/15/5d." As well as being a major importer of Greaves' slates, Hewetson was sold a 1/16th share in the locally built 107-ton schooner bearing his name and figurehead. The vessel was launched at Porthmadog in 1849 for Thomas Christian, a Manxman, who migrated to Porthmadog as a sailmaker in 1843, and subsequently commissioned the making of nine vessels.[72] The Benjamin Hewetson sank some 70 miles off Norway, in 1857, but her crew was rescued by another Porthmadog vessel, the schooner *Betsy* (launched 1827).

The Water Lily

Mr Ior. Parry,   *23 October 1852*
Pwllheli.
    On hearing from you after the meeting that all the owners have agreed to pay their shares of the repairs of the schooner Water Lily, *I shall immediately send you a cheque for mine.*

Greaves' ledger shows that on 8 November 1852 he despatched his cheque for £20.

Jones & Price,   *26 November 1852*
3 Church Street,
Clements Lane,
London.
    Please insure 119¹/₂ tons of slates shipped in the schooner Water Lily, Jeremiah Parry, *master, from hence to Colchester, value £246. The vessel was built in Wales in 1839 and has just been substantially repaired.*

Busy slate quaysides: Porthmadog, (above) photographed by J. C. Burrow in 1893 , and Port Dinorwig (below) photographed in 1896 during the loading of the SS Vaynol, which was built in 1892 and lost in collision off the Mull of Galloway in 1902

Mr Wm Parry,   13 December 1852
Pwllheli.

     I have to inform you that in consequence of an insulting letter from Mr William Jones, Mr Greaves will not act as ship's husband for the Water Lily.

     The Water Lily, 106 tons, was built at Pwllheli in 1839 by William Jones, who combined the trades of druggist, timber merchant and ship-builder. A controversial character, he resigned his aldermanic seat on Pwllheli Corporation in 1845. The vessel was sunk off the Isle of Man in 1864.

Mr William Jones,   13 December 1852
Brynhyfryd,
Pwllheli.

     In reply to yours of the 11th inst., Mr Greaves wishes me to inform you that Mr Parry had the highest freights given for Colchester and surrounding points; and that in consequence of your insulting letter he will have nothing whatsoever to do with the accounts of the Water Lily; but begs to observe that no vessel he has an interest in paid him so badly as the Water Lily since you have had the management of the accounts.
J. Thomas

Greenway & Greaves Bank

Messrs Greenway & Greaves,   4 July 1851
Warwick.

     Enclosed I beg to hand you the following acceptances for the credit of my account [four were listed, totalling £590/18/3d.]

     My pass book goes separately per this post, which I will thank you to make up.

There are several similar letters, depositing money with the bank of Greenway & Greaves, whose name has already occurred in Greaves's letter of 15 September 1851 asking C.H.Hawkins, of Colchester, to credit his account for a quarter of the cost of building the *Edith*. J.W.Greaves' middle name was the maiden name of his mother, Mary Whitehead (1779-1864), who brought much of the wealth into the Greaves family, including the Avon Side estate and the banking links of Whitehead & Co, at Warwick and Stratford-on-Avon. The Greenways established themselves as bankers in Warwick and Warwickshire in the 18th century. From the unpublished diaries[73] of Edward Greaves, MP,[74] brother of J.W.Greaves, we learn he joined Greenways bank as a clerk on 9 August 1819, when he was 16. He was made a partner on 31 December 1823 and soon afterwards took over the management of the new Greenway & Greaves. He was responsible for a £50,000 loss in 1825, on a failed customer, but his grandfather, Richard Greaves (b.1744), made up the whole sum - an enormous amount of money difficult to evaluate in today's terms. No loss occurred after that until 1860, with a defaulting client called Draper. Edward Greaves himself made up that loss, causing him lots of problems and anxiety, as a result of which he retired from banking in 1861, selling his share to his partner, by then named W.Gurney (with a family banking tradition stretching back into 18th century Lincolnshire, where it was eventually absorbed by Barclays). Edward Greaves died in 1879 and the Warwick bank bearing his name became bankrupt in 1887, J.E.Greaves (who still had money invested with the bank) noting on 10 September: "Heard of Greenway's failure."[75]

It is not clear where another brother, Richard Greaves (1802-1870), fitted into the family banking operations but he appears to have helped finance J.W.Greaves' quarrying venture. Early entries in J.W.Greaves's first Llechwedd ledger for 1849 and 1850 show payments to "R.Greaves share account."

The name of Greenway & Greaves was revived in 1991 for a re-creation of the 18th century Warwick Old Bank within Llechwedd Victorian Village, Blaenau Ffestiniog, in which tourists can meander while visiting

John Whitehead Greaves photographed during a family reunion c1878/79. Standing (left to right): spinster daughter Hilda Greaves; son Edward (Ned) Seymour Greaves; son John (Jack) Ernest Greaves; Mrs Marianne Greaves (wife of J. E. G); daughter Ellen Mabel (May) Greaves (later the wife of the Reverend John Clough Williams-Ellis); son Richard Methuen Greaves; daughter Mrs Edith Hansard (née Greaves); son-in-law Reverend Septimus Hansard (Rector of Bethnal Green); daughter Frances Evelyn Greaves (later Lady Osmond Williams). Seated: daughter Mrs (later Lady) Contance Smyth (née Greaves); J. W. Greaves; wife Mrs Ellen Greaves. The child is almost certainly Dorothy Greaves (later Mrs Drage), born in 1876, the daughter of J. E. Greaves.

Llechwedd Slate Caverns, on the land to which J.W.Greaves tied his fate. The modern Greenway & Greaves sells re-minted Victorian coins (¹/₄d, ¹/₂d, 1d, 3d and 6d) which can be used within the village to buy goods and refreshments at Victorian prices.

Williams' Bank

J.W.Greaves did not keep all his eggs in one basket, as we see from other letters, e.g.:

Morgan Lloyd,   *9 September 1852*
Carnarvon.
     I enclose a cheque for £67/9/7d which with the cheque for £15 is the amount of the wages at Glynrhonwy. As soon as you have a small cargo of best 24 x 14 and 24 x 12 you will ship them for Watson & Richards (of Cardiff).
     When you have an opportunity please send me a blank cheque for the Carnarvon bank.

Messrs Williams & Co,   *12 October 1852*
Carnarvon.
     You will please to place the enclosed bills to the credit of my account [three, totalling £983/11/2d].

The £5 note of the North & South Wales Bank, showing the 1826 Menai suspension bridge - which was replaced by the present chains and deck structure during World War II. The bank was absorbed by Midland Bank in 1908 - but the old name survives in the stonework of Midland branches at places like Colwyn Bay and Holyhead.

Williams & Co's Bank of North Wales and Chester, always known as Williams' Bank, was founded in 1792 by Owen Williams, of Amlwch - whose father Thomas Williams had grown rich on the copper ore of Parys Mountain. Its first two branches were at Caernarfon and Holywell. Later branches were opened in Chester (1793), Bangor (1834), Amlwch, Wrexham and Llandudno, before being absorbed by Lloyds in 1897.[76]

North & South Wales Bank

J.W.Greaves was also an early customer of the North & South Wales Bank, which was founded at Liverpool in 1836. Liverpool had long been the commercial capital of North Wales, and the city's merchants behind the new enterprise invested in a phaeton and "a strong horse," with which to send delegates into Wales to seek share capital and customers. The deputation was in Cardiff in 1837 when it was recalled to Liverpool to hear news of the impending collapse of the Manchester-based Northern & Central Bank of England, with its eight North Wales branches, and a note issue of £400,000 in circulation.[77]

The new North & South Wales bank took over the North Wales branches of its troubled rival (which went into liquidation in 1839) to discover an alarming situation, described by the Bank of England's Liverpool agent in evidence to the 1838 Parliamentary Select Committee on joint stock banks:

"The competency and respectability of the people of the branches, I should say, must be very low indeed. In travelling through Wales two years ago I could not help seeing that they were carrying on banking almost farcically, for instead of meeting one's ideas of a respectable establishment there was a small cottage, more like a huckster's than a bank, with BANK written in great characters above it."

It was an era of banking crises and in October 1847 a London newspaper wrongly announced that the North & South Wales Bank had stopped payment. By the time the misinformation was corrected it was too late. Within two days the bank had to suspend business, and for three months the doors remained closed. As one of its steps towards recovery, the bank sold the Ffestiniog, Porthmadog and Pwllheli branches, which were formed into a new private bank founded by John Casson (brother of William, of Diffwys Casson quarry) with the name of Casson's & Co. [78] At Pwllheli Hugh Pugh, who had been a cashier with the North & South, set up his own bank, taking with him many of Casson's intended customers. The Bangor and Dolgellau branches of the North & South were closed permanently, an event which caused a run on the older but much smaller establishment of Williams & Co.

All that glisters ....

Williams & Co had prepared for just this eventuality and when the worried Bangor customers began clamouring for their money, doors were opened to reveal barrels of shining gold sovereigns behind the counter. Everyone was paid, without question; confidence was soon restored and the run on the money suddenly stopped - none but the loyal staff knowing the barrels contained only sawdust, covered by a thin layer of coins.

Casson's & Co was reunited with the North & South Wales Bank in 1875, by which time it had opened additional branches at Blaenau Ffestiniog and Harlech.[79] Having survived seven stormy decades, including the destabilising national economic problems of 1857 and 1866, the North & South Wales Bank felt particularly threatened by the dollar crisis of 1907, with its effect on the company's main business in the port of Liverpool. A solution was found by merging with the Midland Bank, which was without any North Wales branch. The agreement became effective at the end of 1908, when the last Welsh bank notes were withdrawn from circulation.[80]   Several of today's branches of the Midland Bank in North Wales preserve the name of the North & South Wales Bank in their exterior stone work, and at Colwyn Bay, despite modernisation, the interior maintains the armorially decorative plasterwork of its original owners. Midland Bank closed its 150-years-old Ffestiniog branch in May 1986.

J.W.Greaves had been a customer of the North & South Wales Bank's pioneering branch at Ffestiniog, and of Casson's new branch at Blaenau Ffestiniog - and the company bearing his name continues with the Midland Bank, thereby claiming to be one of its oldest continuous customers.

Bargains and Wages

The mines of Blaenau Ffestiniog were worked by small 4-6 man co-operatives, or teams of "bargainers" whose leaders would negotiate with management during periodic letting of "bargains," competing against each other for the price, or "poundage," at which they would deliver their finished slates to the company - the different offers being based on the men's assessment of the potential productivity of the various "bargains" available. A bargain was a chamber, or part of a chamber, from which the slate was to be mined.

Members of the team had different titles. The *creigwyr* (rockmen) extracted the slate from its primeval bed underground, and sent their marked blocks to the surface, where they were split by the *holltwyr,* before being dressed by the *chwarelwyr* (which translates as "quarrymen"). In addition there were miners, employed by the company to provide access to the slate beds, rubbishers to remove the waste so as to maintain each chamber as a tidy working area, and trammers to handle the various railway wagons, some designed to carry blocks, others to contain the rubbish, a task for which ponies were used underground.

Wages recorded in 1850 were: bargainers, an average of 2/4¼ d a week (i.e. approximately 14p), and miners 1/8d a week (slightly more than 8p). In 1860 the figures were: bargainers 4/3d (21p), and miners 3/2d (16p). By 1874 inflation had taken the figures to: bargainers 6s (30p), miners 6s (30p), and trammers 3/6d (17½p).[81]

Bridges were commonplace in the underground workings at Blaenau Ffestiniog. The earlier bridges were suspended from the roof but the 1893 photograph above, by J.C.Burrow, of Camborne, shows the "self-sustaining" bridge designed in the 1880s by Charles Warren Roberts, engineer at Llechwedd Slate Mines. Horses were used for more than a century for underground haulage in the slate mines. The photograph below was taken at Llechwedd in 1929.

2.9% Income Tax

The Rt Hon Lord Newborough   30 September 1851
By royalty on slates made at Ffestiniog from April 1851

April	88 tons	$5\frac{1}{4}$ cwts
May	80	$5\frac{1}{4}$
June	55	$12\frac{1}{4}$
July	52	$3\frac{3}{4}$
Aug	57	$15\frac{1}{4}$
Sept	35	—

369 tons $8\frac{1}{4}$cwts
@ 3/- per ton = £55/8/5d

By royalty on slates made at Glynrhonwy

April	89 tons	19 cwts
May	92	$2\frac{3}{4}$
June	88	$7\frac{1}{4}$
July	111	$15\frac{1}{4}$
Aug	106	13
Sept	105	13

594 tons $16\frac{1}{2}$cwts
@ 2/- per ton = £59/9/7d

30 September, To Income Tax
paid on £55/8/5d	-	£1/18/4d
paid on £59/9/7d	-	£1/14/8d

Balance   £111/11/-

Lord Newborough's agreements are revealed in this letter, with different royalties of two shillings (10p) a ton on production at Llanberis but three shillings at Blaenau Ffestiniog. The variation was presumably based on an assumption that Llechwedd would be more productive than

Glynrhonwy. Among the family papers of Lord Newborough there is a letter, dated 17 March 1843, from Greaves' partner Edwin Shelton, saying they could not continue working Glynrhonwy "under the present arrangements." Glynrhonwy's average of 99 tons a month was, in practice, considerably better than the Llechwedd average of 61 tons - at least for this particular six month period.

Lord Newborough received his money less Income Tax, at 7d in the pound, equivalent to a rate of 2.9%. William Pitt's government invented Income Tax in 1799, to help pay for the Napoleonic Wars, at 2/- (i.e. 10p) in the pound, on income over £200 a year. It was discontinued after the 1802 peace treaty between Britain, France, Spain and Holland, but resumed a year later when the Treaty of Amiens collapsed. It was again abolished after the Battle of Waterloo, in 1815. It became a permanent feature when Sir Robert Peel reintroduced it in 1842 at 7d in the pound.

Lord Newborough

Tanrallt,
2 March 1853

My Lord,

But little more slates can be made from the present openings at Glynrhonwy.

My foreman, Thomas Jones, is desirous of trying for new quarries at two places on the land where he thinks it is not improbable there is workable slate. Your Lordship is aware it requires a large outlay and many years to open a slate quarry effectually. May I therefore beg of you to inform me (should the trials prove satisfactory) if your Lordship will have any objection to renew my lease[82] for a term to be agreed upon (say 40 years) on the present terms. The demand for slates is very great but the advance in the price is scarcely equal to the advance in the workmen's wages.

I am, my Lord,
Your very obedient servant,
John W. Greaves.

Stock levels

The overall position at Glynrhonwy, and switch in emphasis to Llechwedd, can be gleaned from J.W.Greaves' ledger, contained in one volume from 1 October 1849 until 30 September 1918. End of year stock returns are no more than slates available for sale - either a brief period of poor production or a sudden rush for slates would be reflected in a small stock. Likewise superb productivity and poor sales could result in a big stock. Nevertheless there is a recognisable trend in the annual stocktaking. For the financial year ending 30 September 1851, he listed his stock as:

Portmadoc wharf	*802 tons*	=	*£981/12/11d*
Llechwedd	*250*	=	*£235/5/9d*

Meticulous cleanliness was the order of the day in the warehouses on Greaves's Wharf at Porthmadog, with its direct rail link from the mills at Llechwedd Slate Mines.

Maenyfferam[83]	267	=	£256/6/6d
Glynrhonwy	227	=	£234/5/3d
Carnarvon quay	363	=	£462/6/4d

At the end of the 1852 financial year the stocks were:

Portmadoc	637 tons	=	£777/9/5d
Llechwedd	272	=	£326/1/8d
Maenyfferam	71	=	£80/6/5d
Glynrhonwy	110	=	£98/18/3d
Carnarvon	128	=	£174/8/1d

This was the last reference to the Maenofferen operation in the books of J.W.Greaves, until 1975, when J.W.Greaves & Son bought the mine. Greaves had bought Diffwys in 1972 and both were officially absorbed in Llechwedd Slate Mines in 1983, to be worked as a single unit. The valuations listed on 30 September 1853 were:

Portmadoc	278 tons	=	£498/7/8d
Llechwedd	202	=	£311/18/1d
Glynrhonwy	53	=	£82/15/7d
Carnarvon	11	=	£10/18/10d

Subsequent end of year stock valuations were shown for Porthmadog (i.e. Llechwedd production) or Caernarfon (Glynrhonwy production):

	Porthmadog	Caernarfon
1854	£1,543	£210
1855	£2,686	£195
1856	£2,577	£631
1857	£3,433	£226
1858	£3,191	£238
1859	£2,412	£284
1860	£1,248	£280
1861	£1,283	£448
1862	£347	£204

This dramatic photograph, taken in 1893 at the Foty and Bowydd quarry (now part of Llechwedd), clearly demonstrates how three floors, or beds of slate, were mined by alternate chambers and pillars, beneath natural granite roofs, before being opened out to the surface. There are 16 such floors at Llechwedd Slate Mines.

That was the last year of Greaves' production at Glynrhonwy. Demand for his slates had forced him to choose where to concentrate his unpredictable cash flow, in his constant search for new sources of production. He chose Llechwedd but did not relinquish his Glynrhonwy lease until 6 June 1873, by which time the quarry had been idle for eleven years.

Slate veins

In strict geological terms the veins in the Blaenau Ffestiniog strata are the granite-like chert layers of solidified volcanic liquid, which once compressed and baked ancient sea beds of eroded sediment from even earlier mountains, to create layers of slate. However it has always been the practice in the industry to describe the slate as veins.

The qualifications used in Blaenau Ffestiniog can mean different things in different mines, governed by date of discovery, position in relation to each other, and thickness, but four basic beds of slate were recognised in the last century: *llygad cefn,* or Back Vein; *llygad bach,* or Small Vein; *hen lygad,* or Old Vein; and *llygad newydd,* or New Vein. Subsequently at least seven veins were identified, when the various mines were treated as a geological whole, of which those possessing the Old Vein were the most fortunate for this was recognised as the source of Wales's best slates.[84]

The first mention of the Llechwedd New Vein was in 1867, when its slates were marketed under that title, as distinct from products of the original 1849 discovery. The New Vein accounted for £503 of the 1867 end of year stock of £2,167. The remainder of the stock came from what was described, from 1867, as the Old Vein. The last mention of New Vein was in the accounts for 1902, when it was renamed Greaves' Deep Vein. Another bed, distinguished as the Back Vein, was discovered at Llechwedd in 1906, together with a narrow bed called Little Vein, but they were not worked after 1915. A fifth source of slate, the North Vein, was added by surface working from 1933.

Price fixing

(indecipherable) Bristol.   *5 August 1851*
*   There are some very inferior quality slates shipped here, which you would find to be dear at the prices you quote. I understand that Ball & Co occasionally buy these slates and they also sell for Mathew & Co. Now if you can get their slates at the prices you name I cannot but advise you to buy them, much as I should regret losing your custom. Messrs Mathew & Co assure me they do not authorise Ball & Co to sell at any reduction from our present lists of prices.*

Charles Moore,   *24 January 1853*
1 Rumford Street,
Liverpool.
    The Quarry Proprietors who ship slates at this port have come to a
mutual understanding that the discount for cash shall be uniformly 2½%.

This is our earliest reference to a price fixing
cartel in operation among the Blaenau Ffestiniog
exporters from Porthmadog. We know from a letter of 2 July 1851 to Charles Moore, that Greaves
was then offering 5% discount on his product and
6d a ton off the freight charge, but after a rapid
exchange of letters his invoice of 5 July 1851 al-
lowed 7% discount and 8d a ton off the freight.
    The Blaenau Ffestiniog/Porthmadog cartel
seemed reluctant to unite with the other slate producing areas of North
Wales - Llanberis, Nantlle Valley and Bethesda - as we see from the following letter to the manager of the Talysarn Slate Company:

George Bownes,   *20 April 1853*
Talysarn.
    I thank you for your note informing me of the proposed meeting to
be held at Carnarvon. It will not be in my power to attend it, nor do I see the
good that can arise from our meeting, now that the prices of slates are paid for
the year.

    A month after the April 1874 formation of the North Wales Quarrymen's
Union all the North Wales quarry owners met at the Royal Hotel, Caernarfon, to marshal their counter measures.[85] A belief that the proprietors
needed to act in unison, both industrially and in fixing the price of slate,
resulted in the Blaenau Ffestiniog producers forming themselves into the
Ffestiniog Quarry Association in 1875. On 13 January 1879, J.E.Greaves,
who had taken over the management of Llechwedd from his father, noted:

The author: standing in 1974 on the lip of the enormous man-made bowl at Penrhyn Quarry, Bethesda. Penrhyn and Llechwedd are the last of the Victorian giants of the Welsh slate industy, each confident of its future in the 21st century

"Quarry Association meeting at Portmadoc. Reduced prices 5%.[86] Stayed with Ned[87]." That association lasted until 1880, by which time J.E.Greaves was bent upon undercutting his lesser rivals. Between June 1883 and March 1884 several anonymous letters appeared in the *North Wales Chronicle*, highlighting problems in the slate industry, one claiming the price of slates was fixed not by supply and demand but by the major producers.

Another of the letters, mysteriously signed "One who was present," said a meeting of quarry owners and their agents was held in London on 21 November 1883 in an attempt to fix standard prices. "The Big Three, however, as the agents of Penrhyn and Dinorwig and Mr Greaves of Porthmadog were styled, had previously, at a meeting held in Port Penrhyn, arrived at an agreement which it was their intention to force on the rest, and they announced their refusal to be bound by any decision of the larger body," said the correspondent, adding that the big quarries were forcing down the prices of slate."[88]

On 10 December 1884 Greaves noted in his diary: "Slate meeting at Sportsman Hotel." We do not know whether he meant the Blaenau Ffestiniog producers, at the venue of that name still standing at Porthmadog, or a wider meeting of "the Big Three" at the similarly named hotel in Castle Street, Caernarfon, demolished soon after World War Two - when it had served as a store for gas-masks and other emergency items in the event of a German air attack. It stood on the site now occupied by the new offices of Gwynedd County Council.

The Ffestiniog Quarries Association

As a replacement for the earlier organisation of Blaenau Ffestiniog producers, the Ffestiniog District Slate Quarry Proprietors Association was formed in 1892, when the only relevant entry in J.E.Greaves' diary was on 14 November: "Slate meeting at Portmadoc." That association had more to do with industrial unrest than the price of slates. The first Welsh Labour Day rally, held at Caernarfon in 1892, was virtually a North Wales Quarrymen's Union event, and proved a catalyst in hardening the demands of the men. The full story of subsequent events is told in the book *The Llechwedd Strike of 1893.*[89] The Ffestiniog District Slate Quarry Proprietors Association was reorganised in 1895, with eleven corporate members, each of whom had a block vote on an agreed table - not in strict proportion - governed by the number of men employed. The 1895 founder members (with their employees/votes in brackets) were: Oakeleys (1,591/

21), Llechwedd (500/11), Foty & Bowydd (488/10), Glanrafon (410/ 10), Maenofferen (361/9), New Welsh Slate (292/7), Graigddu (220/6), Rhosydd (200/6), Diffwys Casson (110/4), Wrysgan (102/4) and Rhiwbach (28/1). Initially Park & Croesor, Croes-y-ddwy-afon, and Bwlch-y-Slaters (New Manod) declined to join. Park & Croesor signed up in 1897 with 150 employees and 5 votes, and Croes-y-ddwy-afon came in with 18 employees and 1 vote. Bwlch-y-Slaters did not join until 1902, with 50 employees and 2 votes.[90]

The peak labour forces of the members of the Association occurred in the following years:

Oakeleys	1899	1679 workers	22 votes
Llechwedd	1904	639	12
Foty & Bowydd	1896	501	11
Glanrafon	1895	410	10
Maenofferen	1898	433	10
New Welsh Slate	1896	322	8
Graigddu	1898	235	6
Rhosydd	1895	200	6
Diffwys	1900	168	5
Wrysgan	1898	125	4
Rhiwbach	1897	112	4
Park & Croesor	1903	195	5
Croes-y-ddwy-afon	1903	73	2
Bwlch-y-Slaters	1903	54	2

The peak total labour force within the Ffestiniog District Slate Quarry Proprietors Association occurred in 1898, with 4,733 workers. Thereafter the annual returns were as follows:

1899	4344	1915	1224
1900	3839	1916	1030
1901	3438	1917	889

1902	3567	1918	745
1903	3759	1919	994
1904	3864	1920	1467
1905	3713	1921	1756
1906	3216	1922	1938
1907	2973	1923	1989
1908	2561	1924	2003
1909	2394	1925	2023
1910	2446	1926	2068
1911	2629	1927	2140
1912	2369	1928	2149
1913	2029	1929	2181
1914	1757	1930	2092

The effect of the 1914-18 War is obvious. Blaenau Ffestiniog was unique in the annals of the British Army in having a volunteer unit specifically linked to an industry, with the title of the Merioneth Quarries Company of the 4th Militia Battalion of the Royal Welch Fusiliers, and from 1908 part of the 7th (Merioneth and Montgomery) Territorial Army Battalion of the RWF. The 7th Bn was in camp near Aberystwyth when Germany declared war on France on 3 August 1914. Three days later the battalion was mustered at Newtown without the volunteers ever returning to their jobs. They formed part of the 53rd Welsh Division in the futile Gallipoli campaign of 1915. After regrouping in Egypt the division invaded Palestine, then part of the Ottoman Empire, and Blaenau Ffestiniog quarrymen were among the new Crusaders who seized Jerusalem on 9 December 1917.[91]

Rhosydd dropped out of the association in 1914 and did not return until 1921, and then only for three years. Diffwys ceased to be a member in 1916, returning for 1920-24. Job opportunities increased slowly after the war. By 1928 there were only five members of the association: Oakeleys, Llechwedd, Foty & Bowydd, Maenofferen, Park & Croesor. The close of 1930 saw the end of the Ffestiniog District Slate Quarry Proprietors Association.

Quite why it folded is not clear but in 1911 the North Wales Slate Quarries Association was formed as a loose alliance of Penrhyn and Dinorwig quarries and the Ffestiniog association. It was reorganised in 1917 and, like the Ffestiniog association, was also in trouble by 1931. When the board of J.W.Greaves & Sons met on 17 December 1931 the directors noted: "In view of dissatisfaction with the rules of the North Wales Slate Quarries Association, J.W.Greaves & Sons Ltd shall canvass the slate quarry owners with the object of drafting a set of rules acceptable to all, and place same before a general emergency meeting of the North Wales Slate Quarry owners with a view to reconstructing the association."[92] The reorganised North Wales association lived on into the 1980s, when its membership was widened to include the Burlington slate quarries at Kirkby-in-Furness, and the name was changed to the present Natural Slate Quarries Association.

Other stone producers of North Wales were excluded from the elitist ranks of the slate quarry owners, whose closed doors led to the managers' initiating their own organisation - now the Institute of Quarrying, an international body of high repute.

Origins of the Institute of Quarrying

The Institute of Quarrying was formed at Caernarfon, in 1917, out of all the activity surrounding the North Wales Slate Quarries Association. The Institute's official line is that the first meeting to discuss its formation (originally as the Association of Quarry Managers) took place in October 1917, at the Prince of Wales Hotel, Caernarfon - the Institute's coat of arms depicts the double turreted Eagle Tower of Caernarfon Castle. Founder member William Jenkinson's son, C.K.Jenkinson, then 88 years of age, said on the sixtieth anniversary, that the first meeting took place at the family home, Springfield, Deganwy.[93] The last surviving founder member, Sam Richards, of Deiniolen, said on the fiftieth anniversary that it

Regalia of the chairman, and consort, of the pioneering North Wales branch of the Institute of Quarrying.

was he who first thought of creating the institute, while managing Carreg-y-llam quarry, Llithfaen, from where he telephoned Simon McPherson, of Enderby Welsh Granite, at Tyddyn Howel quarry, Clynnog.[94]

"He asked me to come over and see him to discuss the matter, which I did, and the meeting which we arranged at the Royal Hotel, Caernarfon, was attended by two other managers, William Jenkinson, of the North Wales Stone Company, Conwy, and Owen Williams, of Arenig Granite, Bala. McPherson was appointed secretary and I was hon. treasurer - a job I held for a period, but never saw any money because McPherson took full control, and started the *Journal*. McPherson told me the quarries at Clynnog never paid, and finally he left to develop the Association in England. But for my brainwave there would be no Institute of Quarrying, although McPherson would never admit it, and his son [John], who followed as secretary and editor of the *Journal* for a time [three years], also claimed it was his father's brain child," wrote Sam Richards.

Jenkinson (1858-1938) was the first chairman, and McPherson[95] (1877-1957) held the secretary's job until his death. Addressing the members at Birmingham, in 1919, Jenkinson said: "I believe the idea of forming the Institute was broached to our secretary by three of our energetic members about the same time."[96] He named Sam Richards, Owen Williams and Joshua Woodcock (also of Conwy quarry). These names, together with McPherson and Jenkinson, are engraved as the five founders, on the reverse of the jewel of office still worn by the chairman of the North Wales branch of the Institute.

"In October 1917 we held an informal meeting in Caernarvon .... Our next meeting was held in November.... It was then decided to call a meeting at Portmadoc, and invite our employers to attend," added Jenkinson.

Yet a third hotel was offered as the Institute's cradle by John Stoddard, of Llanarmon-yn-Ial, in October 1977, when installed as president for the 60th anniversary celebrations. He said the preliminary meeting took place at the Castle Hotel, in Bangor. Next day a fourth name was put forward by Bernard Hill, executive editor of the *Institute of Quarrying Journal*. He said he always understood McPherson would meet his friends at the Castle Hotel, *Caernarfon*, when they went into town to collect the weekly wages. It was at the Castle, he said, that they held their preliminary meeting which resulted in the first official meeting at the Prince of Wales Hotel, on 19 October (a Friday). Ten years earlier secretary Miss Mary Roberts, who succeeded John McPherson in 1960, said the minute book was opened on 9 October 1917 (a Tuesday), at the Prince of Wales, which was also the venue for the meeting of 3 November, followed by the Sportsman, Porthmadog, on 1 December - which, to add to the confusion, was minuted as "the second meeting."[97] Unfortunately the first minute book, for the period up to 1924, was mislaid when the offices were moved from London to Nottingham in 1977.

Tan-yr-allt

(addressee indecipherable)

Tan-yr-allt
5 March 1853

My dear Price,

    The demand for slates is very great but our prices are too low. I am sorry I cannot say my quarry is profitable but I am still sanguine as to the ultimate result. Another boy has been born to our family since I wrote to you. With my compliments to Mrs Price and to Mrs Baker (when you see her).

Although written as part of the letter book kept at his Porthmadog office, several of Greaves' letters, including the one above, were addressed from Greaves' home at Tan-yr-allt, Tremadog. There were originally two small estates bearing this name, Tan'rallt Uchaf, of 54 acres, and the smaller Tan'rallt Isaf, with 13 acres. Starting with the 1773 window tax returns we turn first to Tan'rallt Uchaf, where the occupant was Eleanor Pritchard. She was succeeded in 1787 by Richard Humphreys, and he by William A.Madocks, MP, in 1802. It was Madocks who, in two phases, extended, rebuilt and re-roofed the house to its present state, for his personal use - installing what was reputed to be Wales's first water-closet. Its most famous tenant was Percy Bysshe Shelley, during 1812-13. The next name we have is Dr Edward Carreg from 1830 until his death in 1842.

Tan-yr-allt, Tremadog, the elegant house from which radical poet Percy Bysshe Shelley fled in 1813 after an attempt to assassinate him - an episode later incorporated by Mary Shelley in her book Frankenstein. This was the house from which J.W. Greaves wrote many letters quoted in this book. The family sold Tan-yr-allt in 1985.

Over at Tan'rallt Isaf we find Humphrey Pierce in occupation in 1773, followed by William Davies in 1778, Thomas Owen in 1796, and James Spooner in 1827. Spooner moved to Morfa Lodge in 1829, and the next occupant of whom we know was J.W.Greaves, who moved in during 1838. When Dr Carreg died in 1842, J.W.Greaves moved into Tan'rallt Uchaf, and Tan'rallt Isaf was demolished.[98] Tan-yr-allt was the family home for the next quarter of a century, before J.W.Greaves embarked upon building two new houses, Plas Weunydd, which still stands at the entrance to Llechwedd Slate Mines, and Bericote, in his native Warwickshire. When Plas Weunydd was ready for occupation, in 1870, he decided to give it to his son, John Ernest Greaves, together with responsibility for managing the mines. J.W.Greaves retired to the Warwickshire he had left 40 years earlier, and relinquished the tenancy of Tan-yr-allt.

The next occupant of Tan-yr-allt, in 1871, was a barrister named J.Lee, followed in 1886 by Lady Nisbet, in 1891 by Mrs Ainger, and in 1893 by General the Honourable Sir St.George Gerald Foley. The General was at the French HQ in the Crimean War, 1854-56; was Military Secretary in Hong Kong, in 1857; Commanded the French army in China in 1860; was British military attaché at Vienna 1865-66; Lieutenant-Governor of Guernsey 1874-79, and retired from the Army in 1881.

When Tan-yr-allt again became empty, in 1901, Hilda Greaves, daughter of J.W.Greaves, moved in on a 21 year lease (paying the same annual rent[99] as Shelley, 89 years earlier). She kept a staff of seven: a chauffeur, two gardeners, cook, parlour maid, housemaid and a between maid.[100] In 1921 she bought the freehold during the three-day auction of the 3,000 acre Tremadoc Estate originally created by W.A.Madocks. The estate was sold on behalf of Ellen Beatrice Davidson (wife of Duncan Edward Davidson), tenant for life, and the title of all deeds commenced with an indenture of mortgage of 17 November 1893 to General Foley.

Tan-yr-allt was Lot 82, sold for £3,700 on the afternoon of the first day, and described in the catalogue as: "A charming residence substantially stone-built and situate off the Tremadoc-Beddgelert main road, with Lodge, grounds and well laid out gardens. It has a southerly aspect, is well sheltered from the North, and commands an extensive and uninterrupted view of the Merionethshire Range. Accommodation: Three reception rooms, kitchen, sculleries, etc, nine bedrooms and dressing room, bathroom, hot & cold and usual offices. Outbuildings are good. and consist of stables, coach house, store rooms, etc."

Hilda Greaves died, unmarried, in 1927, and the house passed to her sister Mrs Mabel Williams-Ellis (1851-1941), widowed mother of Sir Clough Williams-Ellis, creator of Port Meirion. After Mrs Williams-Ellis the house passed to Mrs Dorothy Drage, daughter of John Ernest Greaves.[101] She never lived there and the next occupant was Dorothy's daughter Cecily,[102] following her 1931 marriage to Captain S.T.A. ("Sandy") Livingstone-Learmonth, who became the owner on his wife's death. He served as managing director of J.W.Greaves & Sons during 1968-74. Upon his death Tan-yr-allt passed to his daughter, Mrs Jean Nagy (b.1933), whose home was in France. She sold the estate in 1985 and the house became a Steiner School.

Percy Bysshe Shelley

Tan-yr-allt's most colourful resident was Percy Bysshe Shelley, a 20-years-old Radical under official Government scrutiny, who turned up at Tremadog in 1812, when W.A.Madocks was in a serious financial crisis. The great embankment, or Cob, stretching for a mile across the Glaslyn estuary, appeared to have been completed in September 1811 - an event marked by a horse race, an eisteddfod and the roasting of an ox on the structure. Alas, during a particularly stormy February, in 1812, the centre of the embankment collapsed into the sea. Without prompt repair the whole of the costly investment in reclaiming Y Traeth Mawr for agriculture would be lost.

The huge labour force engaged to build the embankment had dispersed and Madocks, by then the absent politician,[103] was yet to reap some return on his debt. His manager, John Williams,[104] mustered lots of local help in men and horses, some coming from as far as Anglesey, but Madocks no longer had the ready cash to pay for the effort. Even worse, people who had allowed credit in anticipation of the land assets that would accrue from the embankment, became alarmed when they heard of its failure and began pressing for payment.

Shelley, painted in 1819.

Samuel Girdlestone, a lawyer to whom Madocks owed £30,000, decided to cut his losses and forestall other creditors by buying at minimum valuation Madocks' personal estate, including all the contents of Tan-yr-allt and of the Madocks' Arms (now renamed the Madoc Hotel, in deference to Welsh nationalists unable to live with the orthographical problems surrounding the proper noun Madocks). Girdlestone became tenant of the real estate but ownership was vested in W.A.Madocks' brother Joseph, and a former employee Alexander Murray - thus protecting it from the creditors.

Into this chaos rode the young Shelley with his 16-years-old wife Harriet. Madocks appears to have recruited Shelley via the politically active novelist William Godwin (1756-1836), all three and John Williams meeting at Shelley's London lodgings in October 1812.[105] Believing he would inherit a fortune on his 21st birthday (in August 1813), Shelley offered financial support, though as a promise rather than cash, for the embankment and threw himself behind John Williams's fund-raising, with considerable success. Girdlestone (who ended his days in the Fleet debtors' prison) had grave doubts about granting Shelley the tenancy of Tan-yr-allt, which was being advertised[106] to let "unfurnished or the elegant furniture to be taken at valuation." In a letter to John Williams he wrote: "You must take special care to not let Mr Shelley into possession of the house or if he gets in, we may have great difficulties in getting him out again."[107]

Enter Frankenstein

Removing Shelley from Tan-yr-allt was a lot easier than anyone could have imagined. In practice the young poet was deeply in debt (and his coming-of-age inheritance never materialised). He had published very little, albeit more than might be expected of a youth of his age, and was better known to the Home Office's intelligence service as a political subversive, who needed watching during the Napoleonic Wars then raging in Europe.

When he and Harriet left Ireland for Nantgwyllt, near his cousin's estate in Radnorshire, in April 1812, his trunk was held at Holyhead for lack of prepaid forwarding charges. Pierce Thomas, surveyor of Customs, forced it open and reported its "inflammatory" contents to Post Office agent William Fellowes, who wrote to the Home Secretary about the "great quantity of pamphlets and printed papers, and an open letter [by Harriet] of a tendency so dangerous to Government, that I urged [Mr Thomas] to write without further loss of time, a confidential letter, either to the Secretary of State or to Mr Perceval[108] [Prime Minister]."[109]

They moved into Tan-yr-allt at a rent of £100 a year in November 1812, about a month after Shelley's London meeting with Madocks and Williams. By the following February Shelley had completed his major seditious work, *Queen Mab: A Philosophical Poem with Notes*. With that creative task out of the way, and burdened by debt, the secret police, a Welsh winter in a land where few could speak his language, and all the problems surrounding that confounded embankment, Shelley went to bed one stormy night.

"I had been calm during the day, but so soon as night obscured the shapes and objects, a thousand fears arose in my mind. I was anxious and watchful, while my right hand grasped a pistol which was hidden in my bosom; every sound terrified me, but I resolved that I would sell my life dearly and not shrink from the conflict until my own life or that of my adversary was extinguished."

The words are what Shelley might have used to describe the events

Plaque on one of interior walls of Tan-yr-allt, recalling that it was there that Shelley completed his most seditious work, Queen Mab.

which happened in Tan-yr-allt on the night of 26 February 1813, but are, in fact, the words of Victor Frankenstein, in Mary Shelley's largely autobiographical novel of that title written in 1816, when she was 19.

Continuing with the words of Dr Frankenstein at Ingolstadt: "I happened to look up. The windows of the room had before been darkened, and I felt a kind of panic on seeing the pale yellow light of the moon illuminate the chamber. The shutters had been thrown back, and with a sensation of horror not to be described, I saw at the open window a figure the most hideous and abhorred... I rushed towards the window, and drawing a pistol from my bosom, fired; but he eluded me, leapt from his station, and running with the swiftness of lightning..."[110]

That was largely how Shelley had described two separate attempts to shoot him at his Tremadog home, where he had been in bed with Harriet

- just five months before confessing his affair with 16-years-old Mary Godwin, which led to Harriet's suicide and his marriage to Mary. The encapsulation in *Frankenstein* of what Shelley must have often retold to Mary is, perhaps, the best proof of its authenticity, leaving unresolved the mystery of why anyone should want to murder him in the remoteness of Tan-yr-allt.

It is in Harriet's letter to publisher Thomas Hookham, in March 1813, that we find the contemporary account of Shelley's going to bed that night with two loaded pistols. There were two intrusions. In the first the bullet aimed at Shelley missed, while his retaliatory shot flashed in the pan without discharging, though that was enough for the attacker to flee through the window. In the second incident Shelley's night-shirt was pierced by a bullet, and he returned the fire with greater effect. Next morning a bullet was found lodged in the wainscot beneath one of the drawing room windows.

Atop this incline in the open air section of Llechwedd Slate Mines, can be seen the Floor 5 engine house, built in 1855 to accommodate a Robey horizontal steam engine, consuming six wagon-loads of coal a day. Lloyd George's Ministry of Munitions requisitioned the engine in 1915 and removed it (less its flywheel) to the Ffestiniog Railway's Boston Lodge works which was converted into a factory making 18-pounder shells.

The Shelleys moved out at daybreak, John Williams' finding them temporary accommodation with North Wales Attorney-General David Ellis (who, in 1805 became Ellis-Nanney). Soon afterwards they left Tremadog, never to return. Madocks believed the shootings were intended to drive a man of dangerously liberal views out of the area. Others thought it was a self-inflicted plot to give Shelley an excuse for leaving Tremadog without paying his many debts. Even more unkind critics said it was all an hallucination. Yet its retelling left a lasting impression on Mary Shelley, and a niche in *Frankenstein.*

Coals from Newcastle

Frederick Shield & Co,   *18 August 1852,*
Newcastle-upon-Tyne

> *Will you have the kindness to inform me from what port in the kingdom the best steam coal is shipped - to which does the Admiralty give the preference - or perhaps the best test is what is sent to London for the packets. A friend at San Francisco wishes shipments to him on my account. What think you of this as a speculation? The price was £50/8/- a ton when he wrote. Will not this induce large shipments? At what freight could vessels be obtained?*

Frederick Shield & Co.   *21 August 1852*

> *I have engaged the* Ocean Monarch, *100 tons, at 8/- freight, to take the cargo for Messrs Gould.*
> *I am greatly obliged to you for the information as to steam coal. If I conclude to ship a cargo from Newcastle I will write to you to that effect in a few days.*

The 60-ton schooner *Ocean Monarch,* built at the Porthmadog yard of Simon Jones, was often used by Greaves, from immediately after her 1851 launch. She was commissioned by the well-known local master mariner

David Morris, who was also her first master He was the grandfather of Henry and Emrys Hughes, to whom we owe most of what we know about the vessels of Porthmadog. In 1862 he sold her to his brother-in-law Thomas Edwards who, in 1867 sold her to Captain William Humphreys, whose name appears frequently in Greaves' letters. The *Ocean Monarch* was lost in 1872.

Richard Methuen Greaves

"Another boy has been born to our family," reported J.W.Greaves in his letter of 5 March 1853 written from Tan-yr-allt to Mr Price (probably of

R.M.Greaves's first electric power house, installed at Llechwedd in 1890. This photograph shows the dynamo which was belt-driven from an overhead shaft in the adjoining Floor 2 mill, which in turn was powered by an enormous water wheel fed from natural lakes owned by the family.

Jones & Price, his London insurance brokers). This was a reference to Richard Methuen Greaves, the third son (and sixth child out of an eventual total of ten, two[111] of whom died as children and are rarely mentioned in family papers).

When he retired from the magistracy in 1931, after 50 years as a Caernarvonshire JP, the *Quarry Manager's Journal* carried a biographical news item. After leaving school he joined Byer & Peacock as an apprentice engineer, leaving them to go to De Winton & Co, whose name can still be seen in 1997 in the grime above the door of their derelict offices. beside their Union Works in St Helen's Road, Caernarfon. De Winton were then making marine steam engines and R.M.Greaves signed on as 3rd engineer for the 1872 maiden voyage from Liverpool to South America of the steam ship *Mimosa* (541 tons), fitted with Caernarfon engines. He left De Winton in 1874 for a job with Liverpool sugar refiners Leitch & Co. He was offered a similar job in Peru, and was on the point of accepting when family links with the Darbishire family[112] of quarry owners resulted in his being offered his first job in the slate industry, as general manager of Pen-yr-orsedd quarry,[113] at Nantlle, owned by W.A.Darbishire & Co. In 1883 he married Constance Dugdale, of Wroxall Abbey, Warwickshire, followed by a long honeymoon in Japan, during which he found two United States gunboats stranded at Nagasaki with engine problems. Using his De Winton skills he was instrumental in assisting Messrs Whitfield & Dawson in putting the Pacific fleet back to sea.

He joined the family firm as general manager in 1885. In 1900 the three sons of John Whitehead Greaves, and their wives, formed themselves into a limited company preserving the founder's name: J.W.Greaves & Sons. J.E.Greaves was the first chairman (a post he retained until his death in his 98th year, in 1945), and R.M.Greaves was managing director (until his death in 1942). The third brother was Edward Seymour Greaves (1849-1910).

Madama Butterfly

With shades of Cio-Cio-San's marriage broker, witnessing the departure of Lieutenant Pinkerton from Nagasaki with the United States navy,[114] the secret agents of the embryo Japanese navy watched the American smoke disappear over the horizon in 1883 and then sought out R.M.Greaves at his honeymoon hotel.

Still smarting from the humiliation of Admiral Matthew C.Perry's 1854 imposition of a treaty giving the U.S. navy access to Shimoda, followed in 1857 by the Shogun Tokugawa Iemochi's extension of the concession to Kanagawa (Yokohama), Hyogo (Kobe) and Nagasaki, the Japanese were little more than tolerant of the arrogant Americans. Unrest surrounding the naval treaties led to a $3m fine on the Japanese in 1864 and the collapse of the 265-year Shogunate in 1867. A brief civil war gave power to the Emperor in 1868.

Against that background there was no hint of anything amiss with the tiny Japanese navy at Nagasaki while the American

The above photograph shows the ornate staircase installed at Wern for R.M.Greaves, in the 1892 design of famous Chester architect John Douglas. The bell-tent on the lawn in the photograph on page 90 was erected by Boy Scout founder Robert Baden Powell in 1925, as his preferred sleeping quarters while visiting Wern.

Pinkertons were strutting about the harbour, looking for Butterflies. But once the U.S. navy had gone, with profuse thanks to R.M.Greaves for his valuable assistance, the Japanese agents asked if he would help put their ships back to sea. Once again he used his engineering skills to good effect, before returning to Wern, near Porthmadog, in 1884, with the title of consultant engineer to the Imperial Japanese Navy.

R.M.Greaves subsequently travelled frequently to Japan, and when his great-great-nephew David Williams-Ellis visited the country - on his honeymoon - in 1991, he chanced to call at an antique shop in Nikko, some 120 miles north of Tokyo. Opening at random the shop's visitors' book, he found himself staring at the 1902 signature of "R.M.Greaves, Portmadoc, North Wales." Above it was the signature of Henry Cadogan, of the Royal Welch Fusiliers, with an endorsement beside it showing he had bought a sword. The two men had linked up while Captain Cadogan was on his way home from Peking, where he had stayed on with the allied mounted infantry after the 1900 Boxer Rebellion - in which Japanese troops fought alongside the 2nd Battalion, Royal Welch Fusiliers and the US Marine Corps, to rescue the European community. One of the vessels used in the relief of the Taku fort in 1900 was the ancient USS *Monocacy*, from Nagasaki - which Richard Greaves had helped to repair 17 years earlier. Henry Cadogan was killed commanding the 1st Battalion Royal Welch Fusiliers in Flanders in 1914. He was the grandfather of Colonel Henry Cadogan, currently Honorary Colonel of the 3rd RWF.

Today there is a plaque at Llechwedd Slate Caverns commemorating the visit in 1985 of His Imperial Highness the Crown Prince Naruhito, present heir to the throne of Japan. The Japanese link was renewed in 1992 by a visit from His Excellency Hiroshi Kitamura, Ambassador to Britain.

Wern

Much of R.M.Greaves' engineering ingenuity is preserved at Wern, his elegant manor, now a nursing home, near Porthmadog. The present house was designed by notable Chester architect John Douglas in 1892, the gardens being planned by equally eminent landscape specialist Thomas H.Mawson.

He leased the original Wern from G.A.Huddart as a home for his bride in 1884. Joseph Huddart had bought it as a half-finished extension of a much older house in 1811, shortly before the colourful owner, Colonel[115] G.Lloyd Wardle, MP, fled abroad from his creditors, eventually dying in Florence. The house was let to Nathaniel Mathew, and then to his son Major Edward M.Mathew, and it was while visiting this family that J.W.Greaves met his future wife, Ellen Stedman,[116] mother of R.M.Greaves. G.A.Huddart died in 1885 and in the following year's auction Greaves bought the house and spent the next quarter-century buying up adjoining land, which became the breeding ground for the prize-winning Wern herd of Welsh Black cattle.[117]

Beside the house one can still see the rusting remains of his private petrol pump, near the workshops where he used to employ a full-time mechanic and a chauffeur. He was one of the first people in North Wales to own a motor car - preceding his petrol-engined vehicle with a steam car.[118] His dark green car with yellow wheels left a lasting impression on the community.[119]

Inside the high-tech house of its era there is a brass model of his torso, still forming a working part of the central heating system, on which he would drape his clothes after a wet day. Now inaccessible behind recent panelling, but reputedly intact, is the miniature electric railway on which food used to be delivered from the kitchen to the sideboard in the dining room. His very early "Consolidated domestic switchboard and telephone combination," bearing its 1887 patent date, with which he communicated with different parts of the house, is still in situ. In one of the outbuildings his pioneering hydro-electric generating plant is still in working order, though now producing only enough electricity to heat a potter's kiln.

Queen of Romania

Of the many famous house guests at Wern, the most exalted were Queen Marie, of Romania, and her daughter Princess Ileana, future Archduchess of Austria. They arrived in 1925, on their way to the National Eisteddfod at Pwllheli. The Queen dined at head of table, with her host R.M.Greaves on her left, and his brother J.E.Greaves, Lord Lieutenant of Caernarvonshire, on her right. The 16-years-old Princess sat on the Lord Lieutenant's right, and next to her sat his daughter Dorothy Drage, deputising for her sick mother. But for his wife's illness J.E.Greaves would have entertained the Queen at nearby Bron Eifion.[120] The dinner guests included Sir Robert Baden-Powell, founder of the Boy Scout movement, who afterwards retired, in his dinner jacket, to a tent he had pitched in the garden, the Queen's court having taken up all the spare bedrooms.[121]

A daughter of Queen Victoria's second son, the Duke of Edinburgh, Queen Marie was touring Western Europe simultaneously with the publication in Britain and America of a series of 16 syndicated newspaper

articles she had written under the general heading of *A Queen looks at life*. She ranged through such topics as clothes, men and marriage, one article being entitled "My experience with men."[122] She might be described in today's jargon as a feminist flirt, who would have preferred to live the life of an author without the trappings of regality. "Fidelity does not seem to have been decreed by nature," she wrote in an article entitled: "Making marriage durable." She was known to have had at least one lover outside her marriage to Ferdinand I - already known to have a mistress, Helene Vacaresco, before the 1893 arranged marriage. Marie's lover for 30 years, Prince Barbo Stirbey, was believed to be the father of her last

A signed photograph which Queen Marie of Romania gave to Sir Osmond Williams while both were guests of R.M.Greaves at Wern in 1925. Sir Osmond is a great-grandson of J.W.Greaves.

child, Prince Mircea, born in 1913 (and dying of typhoid four years later). The coronation of Ferdinand and Marie took place in 1922. Marie died in 1938, aged 63.

Ileana was provided with an English nurse and educated in England, where she joined Baden-Powell's Girl Guides. On her return to Bucharest she was appointed president of the Girl Guides in Romania but was later stripped of this title by her quixotic brother King Carol, after she had sided with his wife Princess Helen (Carol was married three times). In 1931 Carol removed what he called his "aching thorn" by forcing Ileana into marriage with the penniless exiled Grand Duke of Austria, then living in Munich and destined to join Hitler's Luftwaffe. One of Ileana's sisters became Queen Elisabeth of Greece, and the other Queen Marie of Yugoslavia.

When the Germans forced King Carol to abdicate in 1940 Ileana returned to Romania; when the Russian puppets forced King Michael to abdicate at pistol point in 1947, she left again. She married, secondly, Dr Stefan Issarescu, in 1954 and was divorced in 1965, after which she became an Orthodox nun in the United States, where she died in 1991 as Mother Alexandra, Abbess of her own convent.[123]

There is much confusion in the Welsh folk memory between the 1925 visit of Queen Marie and the 1890 visit of Queen Elisabeth of Romania, better known by her pen-name of Carmen Sylva. Llandudno's Welsh motto, *Hardd, Hafan, Hedd,* is a translation of Carmen Sylva's farewell message to the town ("beautiful haven of peace"), where she had stayed at the Adelphi (now the Marine) Hotel, on the promenade. The 1890 visit is commemorated in Llandudno street names such as Roumania Drive and Carmen Sylva Road; also at Colwyn Bay in Roumania House, Station Road.[124]

While Queen Marie was at Wern, in 1925, she was entertained at a famous concert in the organ room, sponsored by Constance Greaves to raise money for x-ray equipment at the Madoc Memorial Hospital (now closed). The evening centred on 34-years-old Welsh opera singer Leila Megane, then at the height of her international career - born Maggie Jones, daughter of a Bethesda police officer.

Leila Megane

Leila Megane first attracted attention when she won the contralto solo at the 1910 National Eisteddfod, in Colwyn Bay. At 21 she went to London for voice training, and it was there that her teacher changed the unmarketable concert name of Maggie to Megane. The final change to Leila

Megane occurred in Paris, where she went in 1913 to study under Jean de Reszke. In Paris she was given the then cherished status of Prima Donna (before the title had been debased to a caustic comment), ranking with Melba (1861-1931) and Tetrazzini (1871-1940), and the retired but revered Patti.

In 1924 she was married in New York to composer T.Osborne Roberts (1879-1948) - to whom there is a recently erected memorial plaque on the wall of his childhood home at Ysbyty Ifan. Some of Osborne Roberts's best known songs, such as *Y Nefoedd,* and *Pistyll y Llan,* were written for Leila Megane. Osborne Roberts accompanied her on the piano during her concert at Wern, the other artiste being harpist Nansi Richards.[125]

Adelina Patti

Spanish-born Italian soprano Adelina Patti, Marquise de Caux (1843-1919), who had befriended Leila Megane, was in negotiation with J.Ernest Greaves in 1885 to buy Dolfriog, his house at Nantmor. She was then contemplating marriage with French-born tenor Ernest Nicolini, and was looking for a North Wales home. The Patti-Greaves negotiations took place against a background of frenetic property acquisition and disposal, which at one stage gave J.E.Greaves the choice of six handsome homes at any one time.

It was J.W.Greaves who first acquired property higher up the Glaslyn valley from his home at Tan-yr-allt. Simultaneously with building Plas Weunydd, at the entrance to Llechwedd slate mines, and Bericote in Warwickshire, he acquired the old Aberglaslyn Hall and reconstructed it. Seemingly it was all part of his grand plan for retirement in 1870. After his death in 1880 his widow used the house during the summer, and their son J.E.Greaves inherited it in 1887 - often using it in the meantime.

It was at Aberglaslyn Hall, in October 1880, that J.E.Greaves negotiated the purchase of Dolfriog, which he bought on 5 November for £8,100. Next day he installed his family at Plas Hen, an Elizabethan house at

Llanystumdwy, while retaining homes at 21 Marine Terrace, Criccieth, which he acquired on 12 September 1880, and at Plas Weunydd. By 15 October 1880 he and his wife had entertained 90 visitors to their Criccieth home. They were all living at Plas Weunydd in January 1881. In June 1881 he appointed William Roberts as caretaker of Dolfriog, and at the same time "migrated to Plas Weunydd from Plas Hen," - all moving back again on 8 July. A few days later he let Plas Hen to a Dr Roscoe for 8 guineas a week (£8.40). With his mother back at Bericote, J.E.Greaves was also using Aberglaslyn Hall as a home, moving in from Plas Weunydd on 8 October 1881, mysteriously recording four days later: "Beckett departed !!!" When the Parciau estate was put on the market in 1883, J.E.Greaves bought the whole of the Bron Eifion land, stretching from Llanystumdwy to Criccieth, on which to erect yet another home. During 1883 the family lived alternately at Criccieth and Plas Weunydd, but held a garden party for 52 guests at Plas Hen and had summer lunches at Aberglaslyn Hall, but never seem to have spent a night at Dolfriog - which Greaves sold to William Lowson, a 33-years-old Scotsman, on 22 July 1885, although he did not receive his money until September. (Lowson became a JP for Merioneth in 1890. He was the uncle of the notorious unit trust manipulator Sir Denys Lowson, the first baronet, who died while awaiting trial in 1975). Greaves' new £6,449 house at Bron Eifion (which he designed himself) was then nearly ready for occupation.[126] It is now a hotel.

The musical history of Wales might have been rather different if Adelina Patti, still a Covent Garden prima donna in 1885, had been persuaded to buy Dolfriog. Instead she chose to remain at Craig-y-nos, in the Swansea Valley, where she built her own miniature opera house - still standing, in the grounds of what is now a hospital.

Richard Methuen Greaves, son of the founder of Llechwedd Slate Mines, began his own career in the slate industry at Pen-yr-Orsedd, in the Nantlle Valley, eventually joining the family firm as general manager in 1885. Pen-yr-Orsedd was the last of the Nantlle quarries to close, in 1979. The Cornish beam engine, installed at Dorothea quarry in 1904 at a cost of £2,000, remains as a memorial to the aspirations of the valley, though it was taken out of services in 1955, and the quarry closed in 1969. Capable of extracting 864,000 gallons of water a day from a depth of 500 feet, the confident throb of the beam engine was mistakenly thought to be the beginning of a new phase of expansion and prosperity for Nantlle Valley. A decade later, when the time came to honour local quarrymen killed in France and Palestine, the community turned to the lofty engine house, embellishing it with a memorial clock (since vandalised) and an inscribed memorial plaque to which another was added for World War II (both removed to Talysarn church in 1978).

The Great Exhibition

Mr Alfred Ritchie,   *15 September 1851*
Greenwich.
    Ever since the success of my slates in the industries department at the Exhibition in Hyde Park I have had so great a demand for my slates on the East Coast that I have not sought a sale for them in London, but if you will run down by rail to Colchester you may there see them in Messrs Hawkins yard.

Some three weeks earlier, however, Greaves had occasion to write:

C.H.Hawkins & Co,   *27 August 1851*
Colchester.
    I am sorry you think it necessary to keep any other than Port Madoc slates in your yard, specially as I can now supply you with so very superior quality from my own quarry.

Greaves was justifiably proud of his success against international competition at the Great Exhibition 1851, where he received the Class 1 Prize Medal[127] with a citation that remains valid to this day for slates displaying "strength of material, straightness of cleavage, uniformity of manufacture, and freedom from sulphur or pyrites." Two years later he was reproducing the medal on his printed stationery.

Gilmour & Dean,   *9 August 1953,*
Buchanan Street,
Glasgow.
    Will you please to furnish me with specimens of the engravings of the prize medals of the Exhibition of 1851.

Very early in the organisation of the Great Exhibition of the Works of Industry of all Nations - to use its correct title - it was decided to award medals instead of cash prizes. (It was decided at the same time to ban dogs, smoking and alcoholic refreshment). There had been earlier national exhibitions but the 1851 event was the first to take on an international dimension - at a time when Britain was seen as the factory of the world.

Edward Greaves, the banker, made no reference to his brother's success when writing his jaundiced end-of-year notes: "One of the great features of the year was the Great Exhibition in London, at the Crystal Palace. As far as the individual specimens went it exceeded the most sanguine expectations of all, but the effect upon trade appears to have been disrupting, at any rate there appears to have been a considerable dullness in most branches of business and all attributed to the exhibition."[128]

Another exhibition was held in London in 1862, when J.W.Greaves again won a medal, with an unusual collection which included specimens ten feet long and one foot wide, but only one-sixteenth of an inch thick and capable of being bent for use as veneer. The French, who had pioneered national exhibitions in 1798 (as distinct from localised capital city displays), called their 1867 event the Second Great Exhibition, where Greaves won yet another medal. His sons picked up a medal in 1910 at the Buenos Aires exhibition which, like earlier successes, opened up new markets, this time in Latin America where Greaves' slates were ordered for such edifices as the Argentine National Bank's head offices.

The Royal Commission appointed on 3 January 1850 to bring the Hyde Park event into being lives on to this day, under its original title of Commissioners for the Great Exhibition 1851 - Britain's longest surviving quango! The Commissioners were given a supplemental charter making them a permanent body to use the £186,000 profit in furtherance of knowledge of science and the arts and their applications in productive industry. They initiated the present complex of museums in South Kensington, including the Victoria & Albert, with Henry Cole as its first director.

Henry Cole, Esq,[129]   *16 October 1852*
London.
The specimens of slate 6 x 4 ¹/₂ inches will be ready in the course of the next week when they will be forwarded to London.
I shall be in town shortly and shall gladly avail myself of the opportunity of seeing the progress made towards the proposed exhibition.
John W. Greaves
Class 1, No, 216.[130]

These slates were despatched from Porthmadog ten days later, aboard the schooner *Anne & Elen,* in the care of Captain Harry Ellis. They appear to have been specimens for the Museum of Construction section of the Museum of Manufacturing, then being assembled at Marlborough House, St James - which moved to South Kensington in 1857 to become the Victoria & Albert Museum. A catalogue preserved at the V&A records that J.W.Greaves responded to Henry Cole's requests by presenting the museum with slates of various sizes "including Queens, Princesses and Ladies."[131]

Greaves appears to have been confused by a request in the name of Sir William Reid[132] for specimens to be sent to Kensington Palace. A Royal Engineers officer, Lt-Colonel Reid, FRS, had been chairman of the executive committee for the Great Exhibition, and ended the year with a knighthood and promotion to full colonel. Records show him appointed Governor of Malta at the end of 1851 but Greaves was still writing to him in London in 1852. One can only guess he had recommended Greaves' slates for what materialised in 1852 as an order for re-roofing part of Kensington Palace - a similar order was received from the Palace by J.W.Greaves & Sons in 1986, to match the delivery of 134 years earlier.

The Southern Cross

Harry Fox,   *25 April 1853*
2 King Street,
Liverpool.
Will you please to inform me what is the rate of freight for slates to Adelaide.

Harry Fox   *26 April 1853*
I shall load a vessel of 60 tons tomorrow with slates for Adelaide. Please to inform me if I pay the freight here if the delivery of the slates is insured, that is if the vessel is lost is the freight returned?

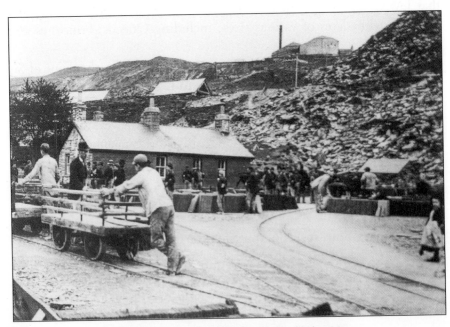

The old office on the Floor 2 yard at Llechwedd Slate Mines.

Harry Fox   *4 May 1853*
    Enclosed you have bill of lading for a cargo of slates to be forwarded to Francis Clark & Son, Adelaide. Please to employ experienced men to stow, and should you not happen to know of any Captain Evans will find you men used to stowing slates.

    This was J.W.Greaves first export to the Antipodes, a trade which continues from Llechwedd to this day. Adelaide was discovered in 1837. By 1845 it was a free port, and once again J.W.Greaves was at the forefront of the development of an important new city, which was to become the capital of South Australia - whose autonomous constitution was not drawn up until 1856. Within a fortnight Greaves was looking for a market in New South Wales, and before long was also exporting to New Zealand, where Greaves' roofs are still readily identifiable.

Harry Fox
                                                              18 May 1853
    Please to inform me of the rate of freight from Liverpool to Sydney and Adelaide.

Railway wagons

Caine[133] & Fallows,   *30 March 1852*
Liverpool.
    The angle iron for the wagons I require is 5/8th x 2 1/2 inches, and the band round the tail of the wagon 3/4 x 2 1/2 inches and the thickness of the sheets 3/8th instead of 5/16th, as stated in my letter. There are already wagons of this description at the Festiniog quarries. It is only the bodies I require.

Morgan Lloyd,   *22 December 1852*
Carnarvon.
    Caine & Fallows, Liverpool, inform me that they have sent some iron per the Prince of Wales *to Carnarvon for Llechwedd quarry. Please to write to me as soon as it arrives in order that I may send my own cart for it.*

Morgan Lloyd   *18 January 1853*
Carnarvon.
    There is about ¹/₂ ton iron come per the Prince of Wales *from Liverpool. Will you please to stop it at Carnarvon till Mr Greaves' cart comes for it. William Roberts, the carrier, is loading today at Carnarvon. Please to see he does not take it.*

Yours very truly,
John Thomas

Caine & Fallows, makers of the bodies for Greaves' first railway at Llechwedd, were iron and tin merchants, with offices at 12 Dutton Street, between Bath Street and King Edward Street, near Princes Dock. Their warehouse, where the wagons were probably fashioned, was at 4 Shaw's Brow, which is now William Brown Street. No.4 was somewhere near the site of the present Technical College. Entries in J.W.Greaves' first Porthmadog cash book show he had been dealing with them since October 1849. Presumably the wheels for his wagons were cast locally, at Tanygrisiau or Porthmadog. Internal railways dated from 1832 at Bowydd and Greaves and Shelton may have moved some of the rolling stock to Llechwedd. However there was still no rail communication beyond the boundaries of Llechwedd, despite the close proximity of the matching gauge Ffestiniog Railway in the valley below.

Gravity incline

James Spooner,   *Port Madoc*
Morfa Lodge.   *September 1851*
    Have the Welsh Slate Company received notice from Mr Oakeley to quit the lands etc of which I am to be the tenant? I am afraid of the time again being allowed to pass, in which case I should be stopped another year from making my inclines.

London & North Western Railway Company's first station and platform at Blaenau Ffestiniog is clearly seen in this photograph, immediately outside the portal of the 2 miles and 328 yards long tunnel ($3^1/2$ kilometres) from the Lledr and Conwy valleys. The station was built beside the connecting incline from Llechwedd Slate Mines, where its opening on 22 July 1879 was noted in the diaries of J.Ernest Greaves: "Polly [i.e. his wife Marianne] went to Betws-y-coed by train and met Mrs.King."

Greaves was, indeed, delayed for another year, as we see from the following letter written to a Denbigh solicitor acting for the estate of Richard Parry, whose land, delineated on a subsequent lease map, straddled the now disused incline from Floor 3 down to the Greaves' sidings beside the main line railway. James Spooner (1789-1856), surveyor and secretary of the Ffestiniog Railway, had lived at Morfa Lodge, Porthmadog, since 1829.

Llewelyn Lloyd,   *Tan-yr-allt*
Pontriffith,   *19 November 1852*
Denbigh.
    My men will shortly be at liberty to commence my inclines from the

quarry to the railway. I shall therefore feel obliged if you will, at your conven-
ience, give directions for the draft of the lease of the land I am to rent from the
trustees of Mr Parry's estate to be prepared; and as I understand Mr Roberts
will shortly be at Festiniog allow me to suggest if it would not be well for him
to bring the draft with him and I will meet him and look it over.

Thus Greaves eventually built his incline providing a direct link into a
terminal spur of the Ffestiniog Railway. It was twin-tracked and gravity
operated, 6 to 8 descending loaded wagons hauling up a train of empties
via a drum at the top, to which was attached a simple friction brake operated by one man, using a long lever. Completion of the incline coincided
with the laying of the turnpike road from Beaver Pool (Betws-y-coed) to
Penrhyndeudraeth, towards which Greaves paid £75 for the cost of bridg-
ing the present A470 road over his incline.[134] This contribution was shown
in the accounts as having been paid by Shelton & Greaves, i.e. before
Shelton left the partnership in 1848, suggesting it took six years to complete the road in 1854. The incline remained in use, twice daily, until
1964.

The Crimea Pass

The coincidence of the completion of the turnpike road from Betws-y-
coed to Blaenau Ffestiniog in 1854, while the Crimean War was being
fought against the Russians in the Black Sea, gave us the present well
known name of *Crimea Pass* for this section of the A470 Llandudno-Cardiff trunk road.

It was a long haul up the pass, especially on a road then comprising
little more than a bed of loose stones. An enterprising entrepreneur built
an alehouse at the summit, to which he gave the appropriate name of
Llewelyn Arms, in honour of the Prince of Wales who built Dolwyddelan
castle to control the pass in an earlier age. Residents of this area were well
aware of the Crimean War because of the very active involvement of the
Royal Welch Fusiliers and of Bala nurse Elizabeth Davies (1789-1860),

who left home at the age of 65 to help the wounded, initially working beside Florence Nightingale at Skutari, but soon leaving - against Nightingale's orders - for a more active role on the battlefield at Balaclava, 300 miles away.[135]

The notoriety of the Crimea Inn began in 1875 when the first Irish navvies arrived to start piercing the very long railway tunnel (2 miles 328 yards) linking Blaenau Ffestiniog to the Conwy Valley. The work lasted four years, during which the Crimea became the scene of regular drunken brawls, both among the rival gangs of itinerant navvies and between them and the Welsh miners and quarrymen.[136]

The navvies remained in the area until 1881, to complete the extensive

Now derelict, beside the A470 road from Betws-y-coed, this old tollhouse was built under the Portmadoc & Beaver Pool Bridge Turnpike Act of 1864 which allowed for the widening and tolling of the crude track laid a decade earlier to create the Crimea Pass. The world had to wait until 1997 for the next improvements, and then only to a very short section of this tortuous Llandudno-Cardiff trunk road. J.W.Greaves paid £75 into the 1854 consortium of landowners who pioneered the Crimea Pass route (instead of Cwm Penamnen) into Blaenau Ffestiniog.

railway sidings at Blaenau Ffestiniog. On 10 September 1881 J.Ernest Greaves, JP, took the train to Betws-y-coed where the magistrates were to hear the annual routine application for the renewal of licences. He returned home to record: "Attended Betws-y-coed Petty Sessions and succeeded in putting an end to the Crimea."[137] The inn closed that night and only its ruins now remain, at the car park and viewing point at the top of the pass.

The London & North Western Railway

Richard Cail,   *15 April 1853*
Newcastle.
    In reply to your query I beg to inform you that I have no communication by railway to any of my quarries, There is a long stem for all descriptions of slates. The present freight from here to Newcastle is about 11/- per ton.

Here Greaves was referring to Blaenau Ffestiniog's isolation from the main railway network which was quite substantial by 1853. The Ffestiniog Railway merely linked the mines and quarries to the harbour at Porthmadog. The wandering labourers who gave the Crimea its notoriety were engaged on creating Blaenau Ffestiniog's first standard gauge link, from its original southern terminus at J.W.Greaves' platform, at the foot of the Llechwedd incline, to the London & North Western Railway's Holyhead-Euston line, at Llandudno Junction.

It was January 1879 before the first train emerged through the ornate Blaenau Ffestiniog tunnel portals, which preserve the date and name of William Smith, the LNWR civil engineer who had succeeded the pioneering Hedworth Lee, at Bangor, on his death in 1873. The first passenger train left the Greaves terminus on 22 July 1879, when Marianne Greaves travelled with it to Betws-y-coed, to meet her friend Mrs King - a fact recorded in the diary of her husband, J.E.Greaves. Other quarry owners had to wait until the completion in 1881 of the exchange sidings nearer the town before they could use the LNWR line.

In a bid to strip the Ffestiniog Railway of the trade for which it was built, the LNWR built a competing dock at Deganwy, in the Conwy estuary. Use of this alternative link to the sea, offering substantially shorter voyages for cargoes to North West England and its canal links, was encouraged by the simple ploy of giving the quarries 2-ft gauge slate wagons, made at the company's Earlestown wagon works, near Warrington, but copied from the FR 1857 pattern. These LNWR wagons were used on the Llechwedd internal railway system, where they were packed before being lowered down the incline for loading, three abreast, on narrow-gauge tracks mounted on flatbed LNWR standard gauge stock. The process was reversed at Deganwy, where the slates were removed from the wagons for the first time, for transhipment.

Deganwy dock

Deganwy dock stands as a monument to the greed and folly of the LNWR. The seed for the idea lay in something quite different: the 1853 St George's Harbour plan, for enclosing Llandudno Bay with stone piers, between the Great Orme and Little Orme, to make a replacement for Holyhead as the Irish packet station (obviated when a solution was found to the problem of building a railway bridge across the Menai Straits). The Admiralty, in its review of the St George's Harbour project, suggested a rail link with Blaenau Ffestiniog "would develop a large source of profitable traffic now taken to the shallow and inconvenient harbour of Port Madoc."

Now a pool of mud at low tide, Deganwy dock was much deeper when created by the construction of a substantial solid pier, 90 yards wide and 230 yards long, to enclose an equal area of water. Ships could be loaded along the full length of the unsheltered western quay wall or from three wooden piers on the opposite side, or two at the end. That the project could never have paid for itself is obvious from the harbour master's log

Deganwy dock, then and now. These slate wharves in the Conwy Estuary were a commercial folly built by the London & North Western Railway Company, to provide a rival export point for the slates of Blaenau Ffestiniog, primarily from Llechwedd, the first to sign up for the new route in 1886. In the above picture a vessel can be seen moored at one of Greaves's piers in the dock basin. The derelict piers are still in place (below). The dock was used by 1,507 vessels of 100-150 tons, between 1886 and 1914 (some importing timber from Scandinavia, others coal from South Wales) but the tail off was rapid: 27 arrivals in 1910, only 9 in 1913.

book, opened by the LNWR in 1886 and maintained (after the 1923 amalgamation) by the London, Midland and Scottish Railway, until the last ship left in 1932. At its peak, between 1886 and the 1914 outbreak of World War One, the dock was used by 1,507 vessels, an average of one a week, but the tail-off was rapid: 27 arrivals in 1910, nine in 1913. Most of the vessels were under 100 tons, with the occasional exception of up to 150 tons, and foreign destinations were rare apart from the returning Scandinavian timber vessels whose discharged cargoes soon took up half the available wharfage. In the early days of the Deganwy venture coal was a major import - from Cardiff, Swansea, Llanelli and Newport - and the LNWR eventually made 2-ft gauge coal wagons for direct deliveries to the mines and quarries of Blaenau Ffestiniog, where steam locomotion was playing an increasingly important role. One of these coal wagons is pre-served at Llechwedd Slate Caverns, bearing the seemingly impossible maker's plate "LMS, Earlestown, 1898." It was, of course, made at the LNWR wagon works in 1898, but the ruthlessness with which the LMS tried to obliterate its predecessor was such that it replated all the rolling stock it could find. It missed a few, including LNW No.158, a 2-ft gauge slate wagon, and LNW No.243, a similar gauge brake wagon, both of which are preserved at Llechwedd.[138]

The parallel standard and narrow gauge exchange sidings on Deganwy quay were intact until the early 1970s, and were used for overnight secure parking of the royal train when the Queen or the Duke of Edinburgh visited North Wales.

Great Western Railway

Not to be outdone by the LNWR or the Cambrian Railway, who had exchange sidings with the FR at Minffordd, the Great Western Railway made their bid for the Blaenau Ffestiniog slate trade. Bala & Ffestiniog Railway, a standard gauge line, arrived in November 1882 at the Llan Ffestiniog terminus of the narrow gauge Ffestiniog and Blaenau Railway.

A year later the standard gauge was extended to what is now Blaenau Ffestiniog Central station, at Dolgarregddu. In order to protect the Graigddu option of using the FR narrow gauge line, GWR supplied 2-ft gauge wagons, for carriage by host wagons (in two parallel trains of three) for the two-thirds of a mile between Tanymanod and Dolgarregddu. Some of these wagons are now preserved at Llechwedd.

By then part of the nationalised British Rail network, the former GWR station at Blaenau Ffestiniog was closed to passengers in 1960, and a year later the line was severed by Liverpool Corporation's water impounding scheme at Tryweryn, a village now submerged beneath Llyn Celyn, near Bala. A rump of the old GWR line was retained for the carriage of irradiated uranium element rods from the nuclear power station at Trawsfynydd (built during 1959-63), and Liverpool Corporation had to pay to link the former rival stations at Blaenau Ffestiniog so that the uranium could be removed, in protective flasks, down the Conwy Valley line.

Trawsfynydd was switched off in 1991, initially for repairs but nuclear generation was never restored and in 1993 the station was officially closed. It is now undergoing the 143-year programme of decommissioning, due for completion in AD 2136. When the restoration of the FR line into Blaenau Ffestiniog was completed, in May 1982, Central Station came into joint use with British Rail, and the old LNWR station was closed.

One-night stand

James Spooner,   *3 June 1853*
Morfa Lodge.
    I enclose your son's reply to my enquiry as to the lease of Tal-y-weunydd. May I beg of you to send him the particulars he requires. There appears a fatality against getting any of the many matters of business I have on hand finally settled. The whole rent I pay Mr Black...(?) for Mrs Oakeley is £47/16/ 8d . This includes 10/- for water and £6/6/8d being 9/16ths of £12 for surface rent of the Llechwedd y Cyd. Therefore the rent of Cribau and Tal-y-weunydd is £41.

James Spooner   *12 July 1853*
Morfa Lodge
I enclose a cheque for the last quarter's royalty, that you may have it when you wish to remit to the Cassons.

I proposed to Mr Barwes (?) to exchange KK for A & B. May I tell him that if we agree upon this it will meet with the sanction of Mrs Oakeley? I told Barwes the exchange must be subject to the completion of the lease promised to me by Parry's trustees. I shall certainly not pay the Welsh Slate Company's solicitor for a deed between them and Mrs Oakeley, especially when the proposed exchange is so greatly to their advantage and they have covered it with rubbish.

It was 1934 before the descendants of J.W.Greaves were able to complete the purchase of the various freeholds which gave them full ownership of the whole of their mining and quarrying area. Llechwedd y Cyd was, and still is, the main site but there was no access to it from the road except over four parcels of land to the north known as Tal Weunydd, Cae'r Waun (in 1840, but known as Cae Drain by 1887), Tal-ar-frest and Cribau farm, leased as one unit from the Oakeley estate. Llwyn-y-gell, due west, was also leased from the Oakeleys. In between were two strips of land, adjacent to the road, administered by the trustees for Richard Parry (Reverend Canon H.W.Haygarth by 1887). These leases were not the main obstacle course which the Greaves family had to negotiate.

Their big hurdle was something less tangible - the shared grazing rights which the neighbouring landlords had imposed by cosy mutual agreement, on the sheep-walk created out of the wasteland of Llechwedd y Cyd (the placename means "hillside of common land"). Still standing at Llechwedd (on the Victorian Village square) is an ancient pair of cottages built entirely of rounded stones, gathered off the mountainside long before the hidden slate beds had been discovered - after which everything was built with the more workable slate. They were almost certainly developed surreptitiously out of a *caban ûn nos* or *ty unnos,* meaning "one-night house." The *ty unnos* was an old Welsh custom whereby anyone building a hovel on wasteland during the course of one night, and having smoke coming out of the chimney at dawn, was deemed to have the freehold with right of residence.[139] At daybreak the builder would stand with his back against each of the four external walls and throw an axe, to determine the surrounding boundaries of the land he was entitled to farm. The more remote the site the longer the transgressor and his family could work undetected to make a substantial house, with surrounding garden walls suggesting he had prodigious strength when he threw his axe. The practice was no more legal than that of landlords who turned out sheep on the wasteland, and bullied the squatters into paying rent for their *tai unnos,* thereby making them tenants who could be evicted.

We do not know what happened to the Llechwedd squatters but by the time Greaves had given the unpromising hillside some unexpected value there was an arrangement between the encroaching surrounding landlords dividing their shared grazing rights into 36 undefined parts, with a market value geared to what Greaves could be persuaded to pay to be rid of the nuisance. Lord Newborough, owner of the land to the south, had 9 shares, the Oakeleys 19 and the trustees of Richard Parry 8.

Flower's beer

James Cox & Son,   *21 May 1852*
Stratford.

I regret I am not in a position to supply you with Duchesses 24 x 12 as I have none in stock, and have orders for all I can make for the next six weeks.

I am very desirous that Mr Flower's new buildings should be covered with slates from my new quarry. I hope you will send me the order for them as soon as convenient that I may be sure to have them ready.

There were close links between the Greaves and Flower families, spanning several generations. Selina Greaves, sister of J.W.Greaves, was married in 1826 to Edward Fordham Flower who, in 1831, established his famous brewery at Stratford-on-Avon.

Richard Flower, born in 1761, became a brewer in Hertfordshire and a pamphleteer against the Malt Tax. He also joined two brothers-in-law to set up a bank known as Fordham, Flower & Co. On a visit to France, Richard's son George met the Revolutionary Général La Fayette, friend and admirer of the young America, who gave him a letter of introduction to President Thomas Jefferson. Thus equipped, though eight years after the end of Jefferson's presidency, George Flower led the family's 1817 migration to the Middle West, where they acquired 200,000 acres on which they built what is now the town of Albion, in Illinois. They rejected a huge marsh offered at 25 cents an acre - which is now Chicago!

Richard Flower returned to Britain briefly, in 1824, bringing with him his youngest son Edward, who decided to stay in Warwickshire - where five years later he inherited all his father's land. He went into partnership with James Cox, recipient of the above letter from Greaves, to set up as timber merchants.

Stratford was little more than a village in 1831, when he built his brewery beside the canal. Sales reached £3,423 in 1833, and had trebled to £10,220 by 1847. Five years later he embarked upon a major extension of his brewery, with a roof of Llechwedd slates, and in 1853 was selling his beer in London. In 1866 his sales topped £100,000, making Flower's the biggest brewery outside the traditional centres of London and Burton.[140]

A new brewery was built on a different site in 1874, and the family formed a private company, Flower & Sons Ltd, in 1887, with Edward's sons Charles and Edgar in charge. There was another brother, Dr William Flower, whose grandson William Flower married, in 1930, Dorothy Drage, of Criccieth, granddaughter of J.Ernest Greaves. Dr William Flower was also related to the Greaves family by another complicated strand (his wife, Rosetta, was a sister of Sir Henry Smyth, husband of Constance Greaves, who was a niece of Selina Flower).[141] Edward Flower was at the funeral of his brother-in-law Richard Greaves, on 4 May 1870.[142]

Flower & Sons was merged in 1954 with J.W.Green, of Luton, who expanded the business under the title of Flowers Breweries Ltd (the apostrophe was lost in the merger). This merger was acquired by Whitbread in 1962 and the Stratford brewery closed in 1968 - the site is now a shopping arcade with a mosaic mural commemorating its origins. Whitbread switched production to a Cheltenham brewery founded in 1760, which has been renamed Flowers Brewery. There is still a Flowers Way in Luton. Four beers bearing the brand name and trade mark (Shakepeare's head) of Edward Flower, are still available. Edward Flower's first business partner, James Cox, declined an offer to join him in the brewing venture, but the timber business bearing Cox's name is still in business in Stratford.

Lloyd George's attack

The Greaves-Flower link was the target of two speeches by the young David Lloyd George in April 1886, first at a temperance meeting in Rhiw chapel, Blaenau Ffestiniog, followed by a public meeting at the town's Assembly Rooms, where he seconded a motion calling for amendment to the much-abused *bona fide* traveller exemption clause in the Wales Sunday Closing Act, 1881. Those wishing to bypass the ban on Sunday sales of alcohol simply bought a train ticket to Llanrwst, and broke their journey at Betws-y-coed, where a comfortable well-stocked bar attended to the needs of the travellers until they decided to abandon the rest of their supposed journey and return to Blaenau Ffestiniog.

The future Prime Minister, then only 23 years old, told his audience the Sunday Closing Act was being abused with the connivance of Tory magistrates who had a vested interest in the brewing industry.[143] He could only have meant R.M.Greaves, a true-blue member of the Carlton Club, and a nephew of Edward Flower. His brother J.E.Greaves was a lukewarm Liberal, and a member of the Reform Club to prove it, or, as the young Ethel Holland-Thomas recorded in her diary for 1881: "I like Mr Ernest Greaves, although all his family are Conservatives, and he was a Tory until he married."[144]

It was at the Merioneth Temperance Association meeting in Blaenau Ffestiniog that Lloyd George first met T.E.Ellis, who became MP for the county three months later. Lloyd George followed him into Parliament with a majority of 18, in an 1890 by-election - and used his maiden speech to attack the brewing industry. By 1915 he was proposing controls ranging from total prohibition to nationalisation of the liquor trade.

Shakespeare's pint

The Flower family founded the Shakespeare theatre at Stratford. Selina Flower (née Greaves) maintained a close friendship with the daughters of her brother-in-law Benjamin Flower, who were friends of Robert Browning and Charles Dickens. There was much literary coming and going at the Flower homes, and Dickens visited the Stratford brewery. Flower's trade mark was a portrait of William Shakespeare, which adorned all his beer bottles, and it was Douglas W.Jerrold (1803-1857) who suggested the association should be carried through into the fermentation vessels. That resulted in their being named instead of numbered, with such appellations as *Measure for Measure, As you like it, The Merry Wives of Windsor*, etc.

Edward Flower took a leading part in organising Stratford's celebrations of the tercentenary of Shakespeare's birth in 1864, when he was mayor. He was assisted by his son Charles who, in 1879, gave the town its first Shakespeare Memorial Theatre. That building was destroyed by fire in 1926. His nephew, Sir Archie Flower, led the fund-raising with which the replacement Royal Shakespeare Theatre was opened in 1932.

Malt and manure

The Master of the
Water Lily schooner.

2 February 1853

Please to buy me at Colchester two sacks of best malt, 8 lbs of hops and two sacks of bran. I sent empty sacks in the Water Lily from here, under Ior. Parry's care.

Captain W.Humphreys,
Dublin.

15 February 1853

Please to bring home with you a cargo of manure, at least as much as you can get of it.

Captain Robert Roberts,
Alert,
Liverpool.

25 April 1853

Please buy me two sacks of bran at Liverpool. Buy two new good sacks and I will pay you on your arrival here.

Charles Moore,
Liverpool.

7 May 1852

The ship Miss Madocks[145] has arrived. The master informs me he has written to you respecting freight to Liverpool - the 18 x 9, 16 x 10 and 14 x 7 are ready on the quay.

The flour will be sent to the quarry tomorrow where my manager will sell it.

Charles Moore

14 August 1852

I cannot send a statement of your account until I receive the money for the last 50 bags of flour. The balance will be about £45.

Captain Hugh Roberts   *13 September 1852*
Edith.

    I duly received yours of the 11th. As soon as you get the ship clear I would thank you to procure a ballast of good manure and come home. The freights here are much the same but there are not so many vessels waiting for cargo

Carl Rindelaub,   *29 October 1852*
Hamburg.

    I have today a letter from the master of the Edith *and trust he will be able to get a cargo at Hamburg.*

    I thank you for your kindness in sending me a basket of apples, a fruit to which I am very partial.

Obsolete terms

    Obsolete spellings, such as Festiniog, Port Madoc, Portmadoc, Carnarvon, Caernarvon, Tremadoc, Roumania, etc, have been retained where historical quotations have been incorporated from the relevant periods. Otherwise their present-day equivalents have been used (Ffestiniog, Porthmadog, Caernarfon, Tremadog, Romania).

    The pre-1971 (i.e. pre-decimal) method of accounting has been retained. There were 12d (pennies, expressed as "d" from the Latin denarii) in one shilling, which was written as 1s or 1/-. There were 20 shillings in one pound, which could be written as £1, or 20s, or 20/-, or £1/0/0d, or £1/-/-.

    The footnotes which follow contain both sources for further reading and additional information that would have disrupted the flow of the text.

Footnotes

[1] Ivor Wynne Jones, *Shipwrecks of North Wales,* Newton Abbot, 1973.

[2] J.W.Greaves' first Llechwedd ledger, opened in October 1849, contains the entry: 15 April 1850, to executors of E.Shelton, £92/2/2d.

[3] The first letter book at the Porthmadog office lasted until 10 August 1853, and spanned 763 pages.

[4] Robert Isaac Jones (Alltud Eifion), *Y Gestiana,* Tremadog. 1892.

[5] H.B.Harrison, *A brief history of the Churches of Portmadoc,* Gloucester, 1962.

[6] There is a memorial brass plaque inside the church for: "William Alexander Madocks, MP, founder of Tremadoc, b. 1769, d. 1827; also in loving memory of Martin Williams and Mary Madocks, married in this church 17 October 1814."

[7] There was a long-standing dispute between the Tremadoc Estate and the Church, dating back to 1808, when the Bishop of Bangor objected to Madocks' having encouraged the Calvinistic Methodists to establish themselves in Tremadog, by giving a 99-year lease at a peppercorn rent on land on which Peniel chapel was built.

[8] The hidden inscription on the east window reads: *To the Glory of God and in loving memory of John Whitehead and Ellen Greaves, this window was erected by their children in 1899.* The inscription was forgotten until 1990 when, while researching one of his "Native Guide" features for the Liverpool *Daily Post,* the author noted the existence, hidden on the floor behind a pew, of a 1919 slate plaque inscribed: *Lettering on east window now invisible behind the reredos which was done by De Vinck, the Belgian refugee sculptor, during the World War.* The plaque had never been erected because the Church authorities would not allow the name of De Vinck to be included, and another two years of negotiation elapsed before a faculty could be obtained for an amended new plaque to be carved and installed in 1992.

[9] J.E.Greaves, unpublished diaries.

[10] Elisabeth Beazley, *Madocks, and the Wonder of Wales,* London, 1967; Henry Hughes, *Immortal Sails,* Prescot, 1969.

[11] Ivor Wynne Jones, *Llechwedd and other Ffestiniog railways,* Blaenau Ffestiniog, 1977.

[12] M.J.T.Lewis, *Sails on the Dwyryd,* Maentwrog, 1989.

[13] Thomas Casson was the great-grandfather of actor Sir Lewis Casson (1875-

1969), who married Dame Sybil Thorndike (1882-1976) to form a famous stage partnership. The memorial plaque to Sir Lewis Casson, in St Paul's Church, Covent Garden, was made with a slab of slate from the old Diffwys Casson family quarry, which is now part of the Llechwedd complex of J.W.Greaves & Sons.

[14] J.I.C.Boyd, *The Festiniog Railway, Vol 1,* Oxford, 1975.

[15] Michael Scott Archer, *The Welsh Post Towns before 1840,* London, 1970.

[16] Once housed at the National Library of Wales, the Glynllifon papers of the Barons Newborough are now held by Gwynedd Archives, at Caernarfon.

[17] Alun John Richards, *Gazetteer of the Welsh Slate Industry,* Capel Garmon, 1991.

[18] Glynllifon Papers, No. 2109, Gwynedd Archives Service. The same accounts, spanning 15 months, cover the laying of a road through Glynrhonwy quarries.

[19] R.D.Gray-Williams, *The History of Bryn Bras Castle,* Llanrug, 1979.

[20] Ivor Wynne Jones, *Liverpool Daily Post,* 5 January 1978.

[21] J.S.Illsley & O.T.P.Roberts, "An 18th century boat in Lake Padarn, North Wales," *The International Journal of Nautical Archaeology and Underwater Exploration,* 1979.

[22] Thomas Pennant, *Tours in Wales, Vol.2,* Caernarfon, 1883.

[23] J.I.C.Boyd, *Narrow Gauge Railways in North Caernarvonshire, Vol.1 West,* Oxford, 1981.

[24] The correspondence was shown to the author by Lord Newborough in 1978, while the file was kept (but not catalogued) at the Glynllifon Estate Office.

[25] Flight-Lieutenant Ivor Wynne Jones, *Fort Belan,* Caernarfon, 1979.

[26] Lewis Lloyd, *The Port of Caernarfon, 1793-1900,* Caernarfon, 1989.

[27] Ivor Wynne Jones, *Eagles do not catch flies: The story of J.W.Greaves & Sons,* Blaenau Ffestiniog, 1986.

[28] Colin A.Gresham, *Eifionydd,* Cardiff, 1973.

[29] *The Memoirs of Samuel Holland,* Dolgellau, 1952.

[30] Lewis Lloyd, *The Port of Caernarfon, 1793-1900,* Caernarfon,1989.

[31] Ffestinfab, *Hanes Plwyf Ffestiniog,* Blaenau Ffestiniog, 1879.

[32] Jean Lindsay, *A history of the North Wales slate industry,* Newton Abbot, 1974.

[33] Red is the term used for what is only a slight variation of the predomi-

nantly purple colours of Caernarvonshire slate, which is from the Cambrian geological period of about 600 million years ago. Some much-prized blue slate was found in Caernarvonshire. Blue-grey is the constant colour of the slate found at Blaenau Ffestiniog, where it is about 100 million years younger, belonging to the Ordovician period.

[34] National Trust, *Penrhyn Castle,* London, 1991.

[35] Ivor Wynne Jones, *Slate and slatemen of Llechwedd,* Blaenau Ffestiniog, 1975.

[36] Reprinted by M.J.T.Lewis in *The Slate Quarries of North Wales in 1873,* Maentwrog, 1987.

[37] Dr. Klaus-J. Lorenzen-Schmidt, Staatsarchiv der Freien und Hansestadt Hamburg, 1994.

[38] Winston S.Churchill, *The Second World War, Vol. 5,* London, 1952.

[39] A plaque commemorating the link with BFN, and therefore with the 53rd Welsh Division, was unveiled at the Hamburg Musikhalle on the 50th anniversary, in 1995, when the author was present as a veteran of BFBS.

[40] The two families were also related: Richard Greaves (1802-1870), brother of J.W.Greaves, was married in 1838 to Catherine, daughter of Samuel Holland, of Plas Penrhyn. See Ivor Wynne Jones, *Eagles do not catch flies.*

[41] J.G.Isherwood, *Candles to caplamps,* Bolton, 1977.

[42] Plas Weunydd (now Plas Waenydd) occupies the site of Ty Crwn (meaning Round House) a substantial house demolished in 1869, having been built up from the thick walls of an old sheep fold.

[43] G.J.Williams, *Hanes Plwyf Ffestiniog,* Wrexham, 1882. There were two books with this title. The pioneering history, published at Blaenau Ffestiniog in 1879, was written by Ffestinfab, otherwise William Jones, who as well as being the Steward at Llechwedd was the highly efficient local correspondent for both the *Caernarvon & Denbigh Herald* and *Yr Herald Cymraeg.* Nowhere does Glanypwll schoolmaster G.J.Williams acknowledge any indebtedness to Ffestinfab.

[44] John Casson, *Lewis & Sybil,* London, 1972.

[45] G.J.Williams, *Hanes Plwyf Ffestiniog,* Wrexham, 1882.

[46] M.J.T.Lewis, *Sails on the Dwyryd.*

[47] In 1931 Bryn Llewelyn, Llan Ffestiniog, was leased from Lord Newborough for the establishment of a Franciscan friary of the Church in Wales. Its purpose was to offer rehabilitation and temporary accommodation of three or four months

for *wayfarers* - the community's name for men forced to become wandering begging tramps, because of the unemployment conditions of the period. At least one confirmation service was held there. When the lease expired the friars moved to Cors-y-gedol, near Barmouth, closing in 1939 when World War Two absorbed all the unemployed. A wood carving of St Francis from Bryn Llewelyn was placed in safe custody in the Church Hostel at Bangor in 1939, and removed to Llandudno in 1973 when a new friary opened in the former Llanrhos vicarage. This friary closed in 1983, when the Ffestiniog statue was given a permanent home in a special Franciscan chapel created in St Paul's Church, Craig-y-don.

[48] Cooke's Explosives Ltd, *Industrial Explosives,* Penrhyndeudraeth, 1925: "Explosives of one type or another have been manufactured at Penrhyndeudraeth, Merionethshire, for upwards of 80 years, and the authority to manufacture, known as a continuing certificate, held by Cooke's Explosives, is one of the oldest extant."

[49] *Florence Cook,* 294 tons, built 1923 at North Shields; was requisitioned in 1939 for use as a fleet munitions ship; took part in the 1944 D-Day landings in France; returned to Porthmadog in 1945; sailed in 1959 for breaking up at Rotterdam, where the hull appears to have been given extended life for inland waterway use: R.S.Fenton, *Cambrian Coasters,* Kendal, 1989.

[50] Webb & Co was headed by Orlando Webb. One of the partners was Captain Wallace Cragg, managing director of Lower Glynrhonwy quarry.

[51] T.Meirion Hughes, *Ffrwydriad y powdwr oil,* Caernarfon, 1994.

[52] Knighted in 1916 for services to education, notably as the first chief inspector of schools in Wales, O.M.Edwards was the father of Sir Ifan ab Owen Edwards, founder of Yr Urdd, and grandfather of Owen Edwards, first chief executive of the Welsh television channel S4C, and of Prys Edwards, chairman of the Wales Tourist Board, before becoming chairman of S4C. Sir Ifan was the cameraman for the first Welsh language cine film, *Y Chwarelwr,* which was filmed at Llechwedd in 1935 (script by John Ellis Williams).

[53] Ivor Wynne Jones, *The Llechwedd strike of 1893,* Blaenau Ffestiniog, 1993.

[54] J.I.C.Boyd, *The Festiniog Railway, Vol. 1,* Oxford, 1975.

[55] The ICI archivist, who is familiar with the files of the explosives division, is unable to offer a meaning for FOF.

[56] Emscote was part of the ecclesiastical district of St Nicholas, in the city of Warwick, and this letter serves to remind us that Greaves maintained strong

links with his native county. Other letters show the routing of cargoes to Warwick was by sea from Porthmadog to Runcorn, where they were transferred to barges to complete their journey on the comprehensive canal network.

[57] G.J.Williams, *Hanes Plwyf Ffestiniog,* Wrexham, 1882.

[58] R.J.Williams, *University College of Wales Magazine,* Aberystwyth, February 1883.

[59] Lost with all hands 1865.

[60] Sold to French owners in 1878, and renamed *Oceanic.* Lost at sea by fire in 1892.

[61] Sank near Cape Clear in 1861.

[62] David Thomas, *Hen Longau Sir Gaernarfon,* Caernarfon, 1952.

[63] Lost by fire at Pernambuco, 1858.

[64] Sold in Melbourne, 1863, and ended her days as a storage hulk.

[65] Lost at sea 1874.

[66] Lewis Lloyd, *Pwllheli: The port and Mart of Llyn,* Caernarfon, 1991.

[67] Z/JWG102 in the Llechwedd papers held at Dolgellau Record Office by Gwynedd Archives Service.

[68] *Independence* was the name consistently used in her owner's papers, but some sources list her as the *Independent.*

[69] Emrys Hughes and Aled Eames, *Porthmadog Ships,* Caernarfon, 1975.

[70] Gimlet Rock, or in Welsh, Carreg yr Imbill; a much quarried headland at the entrance to Pwllheli harbour.

[71] Ivor Wynne Jones, *Welsh Slatemen of America,* Blaenau Ffestiniog, 1993; Ivor Wynne Jones, *America's Welsh Slatemen,* Blaenau Ffestiniog, 1996.

[72] David Thomas, *Hen Longau Sir Gaernarfon,* Caernarfon, 1952.

[73] Edward Greaves (1803-79), of Avon Side, Barford, Warwickshire, died without issue. For access to his diaries I am indebted to the late John Williams-Ellis (1923-89), of Wern, great-grandson of J.W.Greaves.

[74] He was Conservative MP for Warwick during 1852-65 and 1868-74, under Prime Ministers: Lord Palmerston, Lord Derby, Lord Russell, Benjamin Disraeli and W.E.Gladstone. His brother, J.W.Greaves, was a Liberal supporter.

[75] J.E.Greaves, unpublished diaries.

[76] Reg Chambers Jones, *Arian,* Swansea, 1978.

[77] Ivor Wynne Jones, *Money for All,* Llandudno, 1969; Ivor Wynne Jones, *Arian i Bawb,* Llandudno, 1969.

[78] John Casson, *Lewis & Sybil,* London, 1972.

[79] The merger resulted in various members of the Casson family going to Liverpool to widen their managerial skills in banking, before returning to Wales, which was how Sir Lewis Casson came to be born in Birkenhead in 1875, but always protested he was really a Welshman.

[80] Summarised from Ivor Wynne Jones, *Money for All,* 1969.

[81] Ffestinfab, *Hanes Plwyf Ffestiniog,* Blaenau Ffestiniog, 1879.

[82] The 1835 lease, due to expire in 1856, but renewed.

[83] i.e. Maenofferen.

[84] R.N.Crockett, *Slate,* HMSO, 1975.

[85] Ivor Wynne Jones, *The Llechwedd Strike of 1893,* Blaenau Ffestiniog, 1993.

[86] J.E.Greaves, unpublished diaries.

[87] Ned = Edward Seymour Greaves (1849-1910), brother of J.E.Greaves.

[88] J.Roose Williams, *Quarryman's Champion,* Denbigh, 1978; previously published in the *Transactions of Caernarvonshire Historical Society,* 1966.

[89] Ivor Wynne Jones, 1993.

[90] Figures from comprehensive unpublished records maintained by J.W.Greaves & Sons.

[91] Ivor Wynne Jones, *Wales & Israel,* Jerusalem, 1988; Ivor Wynne Jones, *The Royal Welch Fusiliers in Merioneth & Montgomery,* Blaenau Ffestiniog, 1994.

[92] Confidential board minutes, not available to researchers. (This author has privileged access as a director of one of J.W.Greaves & Sons subsidiary companies).

[93] Private letter to Denbigh mining engineer Geraint Madoc-Jones, 20 October 1977, commenting on a feature in the *Liverpool Daily Post* by Ivor Wynne Jones.

[94] Private letter to the author, 27 April 1967, following a news item in the *Liverpool Daily Post.*

[95] Simon McPherson was born in Aberdeen and began his career as an apprentice stonemason in a local quarry, before moving into management in North Wales - *Quarry Management and Products,* November 1977.

[96] *The Quarry Managers' Journal, Vol.1, No.6,* April 1919.

[97] Personal information to the author, much of which was published in the author's "Day to Day in Wales" column in the *Liverpool Daily Post* of 18 August 1967.

[98] Alltud Eifion, *Y Gestiana,* Tremadog, 1892.

[99] The rent for 1812-13 and for 1901-21 was £100 per annum.

[100] O.Wynne Hughes, *Every day was summer,* Llandusul, 1989.

[101] In the Assembly Room of Madocks' Town Hall, at Tremadog, there is a plaque recording that *Mr* Williams-Ellis (i.e. later Sir Clough) "restored and embellished the Hall for its quality and in memory of his mother Mrs Ellen Mabel Greaves, Tan-yr-allt, who died in 1941 at the age of 90 and was a loyal and life-long friend of Tremadoc."

[102] Commemorated on a slate plaque in Tremadog church, inscribed: "In loving memory of Somerville Travers Alexander Livingstone-Learmonth, TD, DL, JP, 1904-1984, and of his wife Cecily Grace Drage, 1910-1952, of Tan-yr-allt, Tremadog, faithful servants of this parish." Cecily's year of birth was given as 1909 in her mother's autobiography, *Pennies for Friendship.*

[103] W.A.Madocks was elected MP for Boston, Lincolnshire, in an 1802 by-election, and held the seat until 1820, when he was elected for Chippenham, in Wiltshire, which he represented until his death during a visit to Paris in 1828.

[104] A very long memorial inscription in Tremadog church, now closed, includes the words: "In memory of John Williams, of Tu-hwnt-i'r-bwlch, in this parish, for a long series of years the faithful agent of William Alexander Madocks, MP, the great founder of this place, after whose death he zealously and energetically carried out those plans which had previously been so ably projected for the development of the natural capabilities of this country ... born 9 May 1778, died 26 November 1850. Also in memory of his only son W.T.Massey Williams, who died 19 October 1856, aged 34." John Williams was the brother of David Williams, (MP 1868-70) of Castell Deudraeth (now part of Portmeirion), whose son Sir Osmond Williams (MP 1900-10) married Frances Evelyn Greaves, daughter of J.W.Greaves and grandmother of Sir Osmond Williams, MC, Croix de Guerre, currently a director of Llechwedd Slate Caverns.

[105] William St Clair, *The Godwins and the Shelleys,* London, 1989.

[106] *North Wales Gazette,* 25 June 1812, and subsequently.

[107] Elisabeth Beazley, *Madocks & the wonder of Wales,* London, 1967.

[108] Prime Minister Spencer P.Perceval was assassinated in the Lobby of the House of Commons on 11 May 1812.

[109] Richard Holmes, *Shelley: The pursuit,* London, 1987.

[110] Mary Shelley, *Frankenstein,* London, 1818.

[111] Bertram Stedman Greaves 1857-59; Henry Whitehead Greaves 1858-60.

[112] R.M.Greaves' senior brother, J.E.Greaves, was married in 1875 to

Marianne "Polly" Rigby, daughter of Marianne Darbishire (daughter of Samuel Darbishire, of Pendyffryn Hall, Penmaenmawr). Marianne Darbishire's sister Louise was the grandmother of S.T.A. Livingstone-Learmonth, who married Cecily Drage, granddaughter of Marianne Greaves (née Rigby).

[113] Pen-yr-orsedd closed on 2 February 1979, when its offices were in St Helen's Road, Caernarfon.

[114] Puccini, *Madama Butterfly*, libretto by Giuseppe Giacosa & Luigi Illica, Milan, 1904.

[115] Gyllym Lloyd Wardle was colonel of the Ancient British Fencible Cavalry, a regiment of Welsh volunteers raised and paid for by Sir Watkin Williams-Wynn, in 1798, to subdue the Irish, and still remembered for its ruthless campaign at Arklow and Vinegar Hill. A descendant of Sir Watkin, 2nd Lieut. Robert Williams-Wynn, was shot by the IRA in Belfast in 1972, while serving with the 14th/20th Hussars. The strange first name Gyllym was the maiden name of Wardle's mother. Wardle was a partner in the Tremadog cloth factory accused of supplying France during the Napoleonic wars.

[116] They were married in 1843. Ellen Stedman was the daughter of a Suffolk clergyman.

[117] Colin A.Gresham, *Eifionydd*, Cardiff, 1973.

[118] Dorothy Drage, *Pennies for Friendship*, Criccieth, 1961.

[119] John O.John, *Trwy'r Felin*, Denbigh, 1963.

[120] Dorothy Drage, *Pennies for Friendship*, Criccieth, 1961.

[121] Sir Osmond Williams, who was present as an 11-years-old boy, in private information preserved by Ivor Wynne Jones, in *Baden-Powell, the Welsh dimension*, Blaenau Ffestiniog, 1992.

[122] Hannah Pakula, *Queen of Roumania*, London, 1984.

[123] Obituary, *The Daily Telegraph*, 23 January 1991.

[124] Ivor Wynne Jones, *Llandudno, Queen of the Welsh Resorts*, Cardiff, 1975.

[125] Personal information given to the author by Leila Megane on 29 January 1954, while she was drafting a closing speech of thanks for a concert by Caernarfon's future international operatic soprano Anne Edwards, at Moriah Chapel, Morfa Nefyn.

[126] J.E.Greaves, unpublished diaries.

[127] Listed in *Illustrated London News*, 18 October 1851.

[128] Edward Greaves, unpublished diaries.

[129] inventor of the Christmas card.

[130] There were 30 classes at the Great Exhibition, of which Class 1 was: "Mining, quarrying, metallurgical operations, and mineral products."

[131] John Physick, Keeper of Museum Services, Victoria & Albert Museum, in a letter to the author, 1977.

[132] Major-General Sir William Reid (1791-1858), FRS 1839, Lt-Col 1841, KCB 1851, Colonel of the Army 11 November 1851, Colonel of Royal Engineers 17 February 1854, Major General 30 May 1856.

[133] father of the Liberal and temperance MP William S.Caine.

[134] Ivor Wynne Jones, *Llechwedd and other Ffestiniog railways,* Blaenau Ffestiniog, 1977.

[135] Jane Williams, *The Autobiography of Elizabeth Davies,* London, 1857.

[136] Ivor Wynne Jones, *Llechwedd Slate Caverns,* Blaenau Ffestiniog, 1993.

[137] J.E.Greaves, unpublished diaries.

[138] Ivor Wynne Jones, *Llechwedd and other Ffestiniog railways,* Blaenau Ffestiniog, 1977.

[139] David W.Howell, *Land and people in Nineteenth-century Wales,* London, 1978.

[140] Whitbread archivist Nicholas Redman, 1994.

[141] Ivor Wynne Jones, *Baden-Powell, the Welsh dimension,* Blaenau Ffestiniog, 1992.

[142] Edward Greaves, unpublished diaries.

[143] R.Emyr Price, *Lloyd George's pre-Parliamentary political career,* unpublished MA thesis (Wales), 1974.

[144] Heulwen & Hedydd Isambard Owen, *My Welsh heart,* Caernarfon, 1969.

[145] The smack *Miss Madocks,* 42 tons, was built in 1843 by Henry Jones.